LAKE GARDA

TRAVEL GUIDE

2024-2025

Explore Sirmione's Thermal Spas, Malcesine's Medieval Castles, Monte Baldo Hikes, Torbole's Windsurfing, Arco's Climbing, and Secret Spots Most Tourists Miss

Grégoire T. Mercure

COPYRIGHT

Copyright © 2024. All rights reserved. No part of this publication may be reproduced, distributed, or transmitted in any form or by any means, including photocopying, recording, or other electronic or mechanical methods, without the prior written permission of the publisher, except in the case of brief quotations embodied in critical reviews and certain other noncommercial uses permitted by copyright law.

TABLE OF CONTENTS

TABLE OF CONTENTS	2
Chapter 1: Welcome to Lake Garda	**5**
1.1 Introduction to Lake Garda	5
1.2 Why Visit Lake Garda?	12
1.3 Brief History and Overview	16
Chapter 2: Planning Your Trip	**21**
2.1 Best Times to Visit Lake Garda	21
2.2 How to Get to Lake Garda	25
2.3 Transportation Options Around the Lake	29
2.4 Visa, Currency, and Travel Essentials	34
Chapter 3: Where to Stay	**38**
3.1 Top Resorts and Hotels by the Lake	38
3.2 Budget-Friendly Accommodations	46
3.3 Unique Stays: Agriturismos and Villas	51
3.4 Camping by the Lake	59
Chapter 4: Exploring the Towns of Lake Garda	**65**
4.1 Sirmione: History and Thermal Baths	65
4.2 Desenzano del Garda: Vibrant Nightlife and Markets	69
4.3 Riva del Garda: Outdoor Adventures	74
4.4 Malcesine: Cable Cars and Castles	80
4.5 Bardolino: Wine Country and Lakeside Beauty	85
Chapter 5: Top Attractions and Things to Do	**89**
5.1 Boat Tours and Lake Excursions	90
5.2 Visiting Castles: Scaliger Castle and More	96
5.3 Nature and Parks: Parco Alto Garda Bresciano	102

5.4 Amusement Parks: Gardaland and Caneva World 106

Chapter 6: Best Hikes and Outdoor Activities **111**
    6.1 Hiking Trails Around Lake Garda 112
    6.2 Cycling Routes and Bike Rentals 117
    6.3 Windsurfing, Sailing, and Water Sports 121
    6.4 Rock Climbing and Adventure Parks 126

Chapter 7: Guided Tours and Local Experiences **131**
    7.1 Wine Tasting and Vineyard Tours 131
    7.2 Guided Historical Tours and Day Trips 135
    7.3 Boat and Ferry Tours 140
    7.4 Cooking Classes and Culinary Experiences 144

Chapter 8: Dining and Local Cuisine **149**
    8.1 Top Restaurants Around the Lake 149
    8.2 Must-Try Dishes of the Garda Region 154
    8.3 Olive Oil: The Culinary Staples 157
    8.4 Best Gelato Spots 159

Chapter 9: Shopping and Souvenirs **163**
    9.1 Local Markets and Artisan Shops 163
    9.2 Best Places for Wine and Olive Oil Shopping 167
    9.3 Fashion Boutiques and Shopping Districts 171

Chapter 10: Day Trips and Excursions **176**
    10.1 Verona: The City of Romeo and Juliet 176
    10.2 Venice: A Magical Day by the Canals 179
    10.3 Dolomites: Exploring the Mountain Range 182
    10.4 Milan: Fashion and Culture 186

Chapter 11: Practical Information and Tips **189**
    11.1 Budgeting for Your Trip 189
    11.2 Safety and Emergency Contacts 192

11.3 Traveling with Kids and Family   196
11.4 Accessibility and Travel Tips for Seniors   200
11.5 Local Contacts   203

Chapter 1: Welcome to Lake Garda

1.1 Introduction to Lake Garda

Lake Garda is the largest lake in the the northern reaches of Italy, offering a stunning blend of natural beauty, rich history, and vibrant culture. Spanning approximately 370 square kilometers, this glacial lake is surrounded by the majestic Alps to the north and rolling hills dotted with olive groves and vineyards to the south. Its crystal-clear waters and picturesque landscapes have made it a beloved destination for travelers from around the world.

Geographical Features

Lake Garda is characterized by its varied topography, which includes steep cliffs, charming villages, and lush vegetation. The lake's unique shape resembles a giant Y, with its three main branches leading to different towns and attractions. The northern part of the lake is known for its dramatic landscapes and outdoor activities, while the southern region is more developed and bustling with life.

Climate

The climate around Lake Garda is typically Mediterranean, with mild winters and warm summers. This favorable weather allows for year-round tourism, making it an ideal escape for sun-seekers and outdoor enthusiasts alike. Summers are characterized by sunny days perfect for sailing, swimming, and hiking, while autumn offers a stunning display of foliage and harvest festivals.

Personal Experience

When I first set foot on the shores of Lake Garda, I was immediately captivated by its crystal-clear waters and the stunning landscapes that surround this enchanting

Italian gem. I had heard countless stories about Lake Garda's beauty, but nothing could have prepared me for the magical mix of medieval towns, lush olive groves, and dramatic mountain peaks that greeted me. This guide was born out of my own journey through this incredible region—a journey filled with awe-inspiring moments, hidden gems, and a sense of adventure that kept me wanting more.

My adventure started in Sirmione, a picturesque peninsula known for its historic charm and luxurious thermal spas. Strolling through the narrow, cobbled streets, I felt like I had stepped back in time. The thermal waters of Sirmione, believed to have healing properties, were the perfect way to relax and unwind after exploring the ancient ruins of the Grotte di Catullo. From there, I ventured to Malcesine, where the medieval Scaliger Castle towers over the lake, offering panoramic views that are simply breathtaking. The castle, with its rich history and stunning architecture, felt like a scene straight out of a fairytale.

One of the highlights of my trip was taking the cable car up Monte Baldo, known as the "Garden of Europe." As I hiked along the scenic trails, I was surrounded by colorful wildflowers and awe-inspiring vistas of Lake Garda below. For thrill-seekers, Torbole is the go-to spot for windsurfing, thanks to its perfect wind conditions and lively atmosphere. Even as a beginner, I found the watersports scene here exhilarating, with expert instructors eager to share their passion for the lake.

The charming town of Arco, famous for its rock climbing opportunities, was another unexpected delight. Scaling the limestone cliffs, I was rewarded with stunning views of the lake and surrounding countryside. But what truly set this trip apart were the hidden spots I discovered along the way—secluded beaches, secret viewpoints, and charming trattorias that serve the most delicious local dishes. These are the places that most guides miss, but they are the true soul of Lake Garda.

This guide goes beyond the typical tourist hotspots to give you an insider's perspective on Lake Garda. Whether you're a family looking for fun activities, a couple seeking romance, or an adventurer eager to explore the great outdoors, this guide has something for everyone. Get ready to dive into the heart of Italy's largest lake and uncover the experiences that will make your trip to Lake Garda truly unforgettable.

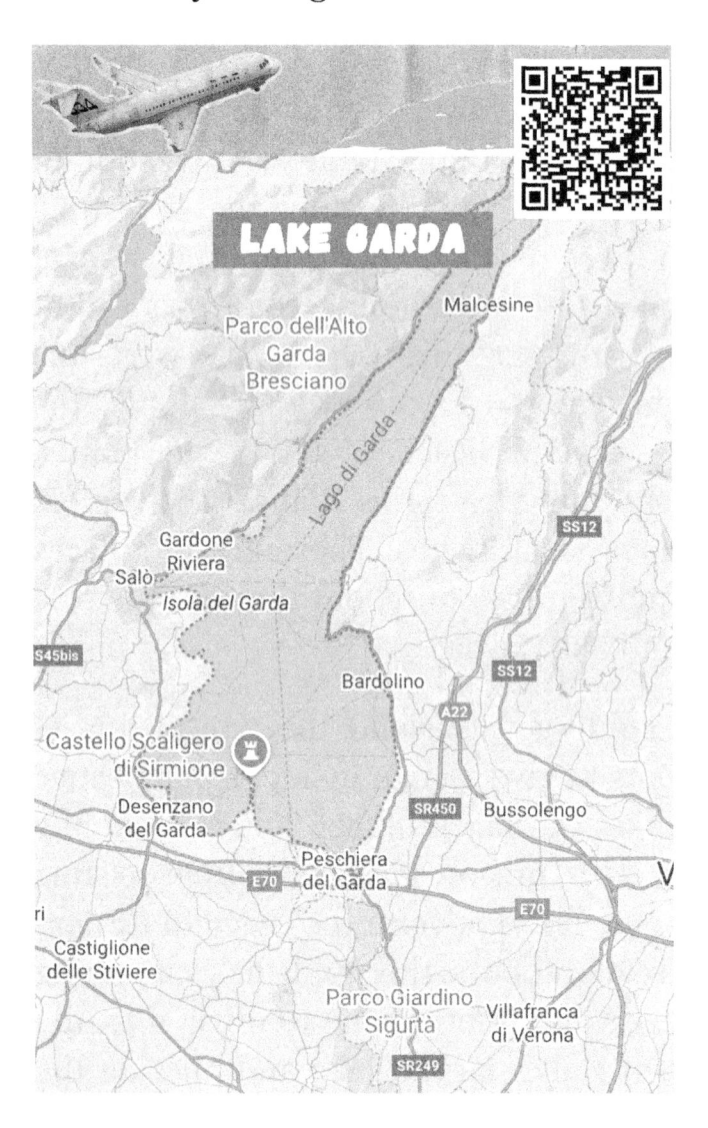

1.2 Why Visit Lake Garda?

Lake Garda is a destination that offers a unique blend of natural beauty, cultural richness, and a plethora of activities, making it an ideal choice for travelers of all types. Here are several compelling reasons to choose Lake Garda for your next getaway:

1. Stunning Natural Scenery

The breathtaking landscapes surrounding Lake Garda are nothing short of spectacular. From the crystal-clear waters reflecting the sky to the dramatic mountain backdrops, the lake provides a picturesque setting for photography, relaxation, and outdoor exploration. The diverse ecosystems, including lush forests and charming gardens, create a serene environment that invites visitors to unwind and reconnect with nature.

2. Rich Cultural Heritage

Lake Garda is steeped in history and culture. The region boasts a wealth of historical sites, including ancient castles, Roman ruins, and charming medieval towns. Visitors can explore Sirmione's Scaliger Castle, wander through the narrow streets of Malcesine, or admire the frescoes in the churches of Riva del Garda. Each town has its own unique story, allowing travelers to immerse themselves in the cultural tapestry of the area.

3. Outdoor Activities for Everyone

Whether you're an adrenaline junkie or prefer leisurely pursuits, Lake Garda has something for everyone:
- **Water Sports:** Enjoy sailing, windsurfing, and kayaking on the lake's tranquil waters.
- **Hiking and Biking:** Explore the numerous trails that wind through the hills and mountains, offering breathtaking views and varying levels of difficulty.

- **Adventure Sports:** For thrill-seekers, options like rock climbing, paragliding, and mountain biking are readily available.

4. Culinary Delights

Lake Garda is renowned for its exquisite cuisine, featuring fresh local ingredients and traditional recipes. Indulge in regional dishes such as:

- **Risotto with Fresh Fish:** A local specialty that highlights the lake's bounty.
- **Olive Oil:** Sample some of the finest extra virgin olive oils produced in the region.
- **Wine:** Enjoy tastings at local vineyards, where you can savor the famous Bardolino and Valpolicella wines.

5. Family-Friendly Destination

Lake Garda is a fantastic destination for families, offering a wide range of activities that cater to all ages. From amusement parks like Gardaland to interactive museums and outdoor adventures, families can create unforgettable memories together.

The safe and welcoming atmosphere makes it easy for families to explore and enjoy their time by the lake.

6. Accessibility

Located just a short drive from major cities like Milan, Verona, and Venice, Lake Garda is easily accessible for travelers. The region is well-connected by public transportation, making it convenient to explore neighboring towns and attractions. This accessibility allows visitors to experience the beauty of Lake Garda alongside other iconic Italian destinations.

7. Year-Round Appeal

Unlike many tourist destinations that are limited to a specific season, Lake Garda offers activities and attractions year-round. Summer is perfect for water sports and sunbathing, while autumn celebrates harvest festivals and wine tastings. Winter brings opportunities for skiing in the nearby mountains, and spring showcases blooming landscapes and outdoor festivals.

With its stunning scenery, rich cultural heritage, diverse activities, and culinary delights, Lake Garda is a must-visit destination for anyone seeking an unforgettable experience in Italy. Whether you're traveling solo, as a couple, or with family, this enchanting lake promises to leave you with lasting memories and a desire to return.

1.3 Brief History and Overview

Lake Garda has a rich and diverse history that spans thousands of years, shaped by various cultures and civilizations. Here's a concise overview of its historical journey:

Prehistoric Era

The region around Lake Garda has been inhabited since prehistoric times, with evidence of human settlements dating back to the Bronze Age. Archaeological findings, including tools and artifacts, indicate that early inhabitants engaged in fishing and agriculture, utilizing the lake's abundant resources.

Roman Influence

During the Roman Empire, Lake Garda became an important strategic and economic hub. The Romans built villas, roads, and towns around the lake, enhancing its connectivity and prosperity. Towns like Sirmione and Desenzano del Garda were established as key points for trade and military operations. The remnants of Roman architecture, including ruins and ancient roads, can still be seen today.

Medieval Period

The fall of the Roman Empire led to a new chapter in the region's history. Throughout the Middle Ages, Lake Garda was influenced by various powers, including the Lombards and the Franks. The establishment of fortified castles, such as the Scaliger Castle in Sirmione, reflects the need for defense against invasions. This era also saw the rise of small independent municipalities, each with its own governance and cultural identity.

Renaissance and Beyond

The Renaissance brought a flourishing of arts and culture to the region. Wealthy families commissioned beautiful villas and palaces, many of which still stand today as testaments to this golden age. Additionally, the lake became a popular retreat for artists and intellectuals, drawn by its stunning landscapes and tranquil environment.

19th and 20th Centuries

The 19th century marked the beginning of tourism in Lake Garda, spurred by the advent of the railway and improved transportation. The region became a favored destination for European aristocrats and tourists, leading to the development of hotels, resorts, and recreational activities.

The beautiful landscapes and mild climate contributed to its popularity.

Modern Era

Today, Lake Garda is renowned as one of Italy's premier tourist destinations. It attracts millions of visitors each year, offering a unique blend of natural beauty, cultural heritage, and outdoor activities. The local economy is heavily reliant on tourism, with an emphasis on sustainable practices to preserve the region's natural resources and charm.

Lake Garda's history is a fascinating tapestry woven from various cultures, each leaving its mark on the landscape and its people. From prehistoric settlements to a modern tourist hotspot, the lake continues to enchant visitors with its beauty and rich historical significance. Exploring its towns and landmarks offers an opportunity to delve into this captivating history, making your visit to Lake Garda all the more enriching.

Chapter 2: Planning Your Trip

2.1 Best Times to Visit Lake Garda

Choosing the right time to visit Lake Garda can significantly enhance your experience. The region boasts a Mediterranean climate, which means it offers a variety of seasonal attractions. Here's a breakdown of the best times to visit, along with what you can expect during each season.

Spring (March to May)

Overview: Spring is one of the most beautiful times to visit Lake Garda. As the weather warms up, the landscape comes alive with blooming flowers and lush greenery.
- **Weather:** Temperatures range from 10°C to 20°C (50°F to 68°F), making it pleasantly mild.

- **Activities:** Spring is perfect for hiking, cycling, and exploring the towns without the summer crowds. Local festivals, such as the olive blossom festival, celebrate the region's agricultural heritage.
- **Pros:** Fewer tourists, vibrant nature, and cultural events.
- **Cons:** Some attractions may have limited hours or be closed for maintenance.

Summer (June to August)

Overview: Summer is peak tourist season at Lake Garda, attracting visitors from around the world drawn by the warm weather and vibrant atmosphere.
- **Weather:** Expect warm to hot temperatures, ranging from 20°C to 35°C (68°F to 95°F). The lake offers refreshing relief from the heat.
- **Activities:** Ideal for water sports, sunbathing, and outdoor festivals. Popular events include the Bardolino Wine Festival and various music festivals.

- **Pros:** All attractions are open, and there are numerous outdoor activities and events.
- **Cons:** Crowded tourist spots, higher prices for accommodations, and potential for hot weather.

Autumn (September to November)

Overview: Autumn is a wonderful time to visit Lake Garda, as the summer crowds dissipate and the landscape transforms with vibrant fall colors.

- **Weather:** Temperatures gradually cool down, ranging from 15°C to 25°C (59°F to 77°F) in September, dropping further in October and November.
- **Activities:** Enjoy hiking, wine-tasting tours during the grape harvest season, and local food festivals celebrating seasonal produce.
- **Pros:** Mild weather, fewer tourists, and beautiful autumn foliage.
- **Cons:** Some attractions may begin to close for the season as November approaches.

Winter (December to February)

Overview: Winter at Lake Garda is quieter but equally enchanting, particularly for those who enjoy a peaceful retreat.

- **Weather:** Temperatures range from 0°C to 10°C (32°F to 50°F), with the possibility of frost, particularly in the northern areas.
- **Activities:** While water activities are not feasible, you can enjoy winter sports in the nearby mountains, visit Christmas markets, and explore the charming towns adorned with festive decorations.
- **Pros:** Tranquility, picturesque winter scenery, and lower prices for accommodations.
- **Cons:** Limited outdoor activities, and some attractions may be closed during the off-season.

The best time to visit Lake Garda ultimately depends on your preferences and the type of experience you seek. Whether you're drawn to the vibrant life of summer, the blooming beauty of spring, the colorful tranquility of autumn, or the serene charm of winter, Lake Garda has something to offer year-round. Planning your visit around these seasonal highlights will help you make the most of your trip to this breathtaking destination.

2.2 How to Get to Lake Garda

Reaching Lake Garda is relatively straightforward, thanks to its convenient location and well-developed transportation infrastructure. Here's a comprehensive guide on how to get to this stunning destination, whether you're traveling by air, train, or car.

By Air

Nearest Airports:
- **Verona Villafranca Airport (VRN):** Located approximately 30 kilometers (18 miles) from the lake, this is the most convenient airport for accessing Lake Garda.
- **Bergamo Orio al Serio Airport (BGY):** About 90 kilometers (56 miles)

away, this airport also serves numerous low-cost airlines.

- **Milan Malpensa Airport (MXP):** Approximately 150 kilometers (93 miles) from Lake Garda, it is a major international airport with more flight options.

Transportation from Airports:

- **Shuttle Services:** Many shuttle services operate between the airports and various towns around Lake Garda.

- **Car Rentals:** Renting a car is a popular option for those who want the flexibility to explore the region at their own pace.

- **Public Transport:** Buses and trains connect airports to nearby towns. For example, from Verona Airport, you can take a bus to Verona and then a train to Desenzano del Garda.

By Train

Lake Garda is well-connected by the Italian railway system, making train travel a convenient option.

Main Train Stations:

- **Desenzano del Garda:** The largest station on the lake, with frequent trains from major cities like Milan, Verona, and Venice.

- **Peschiera del Garda:** Another key station with good connections, particularly for visitors heading to the southern part of the lake.

- **Riva del Garda:** Although there is no direct train service to Riva, you can take a train to Rovereto and then a bus.

Tips:

- Check train schedules in advance, especially during holidays or peak seasons.
- Consider purchasing a rail pass if you plan to travel extensively by train through Italy.

By Car

Driving to Lake Garda offers the freedom to explore the scenic routes and surrounding areas.

Major Highways:

- **A4 Autostrada:** This highway connects Milan to Venice and has several exits for towns around Lake Garda, such as Desenzano and Peschiera.

- **SS450 and SS237:** These roads provide access to the northern part of the lake, leading to towns like Riva del Garda and Torbole.

Parking:

- Most towns have designated parking areas, but be prepared for potential fees. Some areas may have limited parking availability, especially during peak tourist seasons.

By Bus

Buses are a cost-effective way to reach Lake Garda from nearby cities.

Bus Services:

- Regular bus services operate from cities like Verona, Milan, and Brescia to various towns around the lake.
- Check local bus schedules (e.g., FlixBus) for routes and frequency.

Getting to Lake Garda is easy, whether you choose to fly, take a train, drive, or travel by bus. Each mode of transportation offers its own advantages, and the choice largely depends on your travel preferences and itinerary. Once you arrive, you'll find that the lake's beauty and charm are well worth the journey.

2.3 Transportation Options Around the Lake

Once you arrive at Lake Garda, getting around the area is convenient and offers various options to explore its stunning towns and landscapes. Here's a comprehensive overview of transportation methods available around the lake.

1. Car Rental

Overview: Renting a car provides the greatest flexibility to explore Lake Garda and its surroundings at your own pace.
- **Availability:** Car rental agencies are available at airports and in major towns.
- **Road Conditions:** Roads around the lake are generally well-maintained, though some can be narrow and winding, especially in the northern areas.
- **Parking:** Most towns have parking facilities, but availability can vary, particularly in peak tourist seasons.

2. Public Buses

Overview: The bus system around Lake Garda is extensive and connects many towns and attractions.
- **Bus Services:** The main operator is Trasporti Pubblici di Brescia, which provides regular services between towns like Desenzano, Peschiera, Sirmione, and Riva del Garda.

- **Tickets:** Tickets can be purchased at kiosks or on board (though it's advisable to buy in advance to avoid higher on-board fees).
- **Pros:** Affordable and convenient for reaching towns not easily accessible by other means.

3. Ferries and Boats

Overview: Traveling by ferry or boat offers a scenic way to see the lake and its charming towns.

- **Ferry Services:** Various companies operate ferry services, including Navigazione Lago di Garda, connecting major towns like Limone, Malcesine, and Bardolino.
- **Types of Boats:** Options range from high-speed ferries to traditional boats, providing different experiences.
- **Schedules:** Ferries typically run more frequently during the summer months. Check schedules in advance, especially in the off-season.

4. Bicycles

Overview: Cycling is a popular way to explore the lake, with many dedicated bike paths available.
- **Bike Rentals:** Numerous rental shops are located in towns around the lake, offering standard and electric bikes.
- **Cycling Routes:** The lake features a variety of trails catering to different skill levels, including scenic routes along the shoreline and more challenging paths in the hills.
- **Pros:** Eco-friendly and allows for a closer connection to the beautiful surroundings.

5. Walking

Overview: Many towns around Lake Garda are pedestrian-friendly, making walking a pleasant way to explore.

- **Scenic Strolls:** Enjoy lakeside promenades and charming streets filled with shops and cafes.

- **Hiking:** There are numerous hiking trails in the surrounding hills and mountains, offering stunning views of the lake.

6. Taxis and Ride-Sharing

Overview: Taxis are available in most towns, and ride-sharing services like Uber may be accessible in some areas.
- **Taxis:** Easily found at taxi stands or can be booked via phone.
- **Pros:** Convenient for short distances or when public transport is less frequent.

Lake Garda offers a variety of transportation options to suit every traveler's needs. Whether you choose to rent a car for flexibility, utilize public transport for convenience, or embrace the scenic beauty by ferry or bicycle, you'll find it easy to explore the lake and its enchanting towns. Each mode of transportation provides a unique way to experience the breathtaking landscapes and rich culture of this stunning region.

2.4 Visa, Currency, and Travel Essentials

When planning your trip to Lake Garda, it's important to consider the necessary travel documentation, currency, and essential items to ensure a smooth and enjoyable experience. Here's what you need to know:

1. Visa Requirements

Overview: Visa requirements for Italy depend on your nationality.
- **Schengen Area:** Citizens of EU member countries and Schengen Area countries do not need a visa to enter Italy.
- **Non-EU Visitors:** Many countries, including the USA, Canada, Australia, and several others, can enter Italy for tourism without a visa for stays up to 90 days. Check the specific regulations for your country before traveling.
- **Longer Stays:** If you plan to stay longer than 90 days, you will need to apply for a visa in advance.

2. Currency

Overview: Italy uses the Euro (€) as its official currency.

- **Currency Exchange:** You can exchange currency at banks, exchange offices, and airports. ATMs are widely available and often provide better rates than currency exchange services.
- **Credit and Debit Cards:** Most establishments, including hotels, restaurants, and shops, accept credit and debit cards. However, it's advisable to carry some cash for smaller vendors and markets.

3. Travel Essentials

Overview: Preparing for your trip includes packing essential items and being aware of local customs.

Health and Safety
- **Travel Insurance:** Consider purchasing travel insurance to cover medical

emergencies, trip cancellations, and lost belongings.
- **Health Precautions:** Check if any vaccinations are recommended or required before traveling. Make sure to carry any necessary medications with you.

Electrical Outlets
- **Voltage:** Italy operates on a 230V supply voltage and uses Type C, F, and L plugs. Bring a universal adapter if your devices use a different plug type.

Local Customs
- **Language:** While Italian is the official language, many people in tourist areas speak English. Learning a few basic Italian phrases can enhance your experience.
- **Tipping:** Tipping is appreciated but not mandatory. In restaurants, rounding up the bill or leaving small change is common.

Clothing and Gear
- **Seasonal Clothing:** Pack according to the season. Summers are warm, so light

clothing is appropriate, while winters can be cold, requiring warmer attire.

- **Comfortable Shoes:** Bring comfortable walking shoes for exploring towns and hiking trails.

Documentation

- **Passport:** Ensure your passport is valid for at least six months beyond your planned departure date.

- **Copies of Important Documents:** Keep photocopies of your passport, visa (if required), travel insurance, and other important documents in a safe place.

Being informed about visa requirements, currency, and travel essentials will help ensure a hassle-free trip to Lake Garda. By preparing in advance, you can focus on enjoying the breathtaking scenery, rich culture, and memorable experiences that this beautiful region has to offer.

Chapter 3: Where to Stay

3.1 Top Resorts and Hotels by the Lake

Choosing the right accommodation can greatly enhance your experience at Lake Garda. The region offers a wide range of options, from luxurious resorts to charming boutique hotels, catering to different tastes and budgets. Here's a detailed look at some of the top resorts and hotels by the lake.

1. Aqualux Hotel & Spa Bardolino

Overview: This luxurious hotel is situated in Bardolino, featuring a stunning design that blends seamlessly with the natural surroundings.

- Amenities:
   - Extensive spa facilities with wellness treatments, sauna, and indoor/outdoor pools.

- Multiple dining options, including a gourmet restaurant and casual eateries.

- Direct access to the lake and private beach area.

- Highlights:

- Eco-friendly design with a focus on sustainability.

- Ideal for couples looking for a romantic getaway or wellness retreat.

2. Grand Hotel Terme

Overview: Located in Sirmione, this elegant hotel is renowned for its thermal spa and beautiful lakeside views.

- Amenities:
   - Thermal baths and wellness center offering a variety of treatments.
   - Fine dining restaurant with a focus on local cuisine.
   - Outdoor swimming pool and private beach access.

- Highlights:
   - Historic building with luxurious interiors and a prime location near the famous Scaliger Castle.
   - Perfect for those seeking relaxation and pampering.

3. Hotel Villa del Sogno

Overview: Nestled in Gardone Riviera, this charming boutique hotel offers a blend of history and modern comfort.

- Amenities:
   - Beautifully landscaped gardens with stunning views of the lake.

- Outdoor swimming pool and terrace for sunbathing.
 - On-site restaurant serving traditional Italian dishes.

- **Highlights:**
 - Rich history, having been a favorite among artists and writers.
 - Intimate atmosphere, ideal for romantic escapes and quiet retreats.

4. Hotel Casa Barca

Overview: Located in the tranquil area of Torri del Benaco, this family-run hotel offers a welcoming atmosphere and beautiful lake views.

- **Amenities:**
 - Outdoor swimming pool with a sun terrace.
 - Complimentary bicycles for exploring the surrounding area.
 - On-site bar and breakfast service.

- Highlights:
  - Friendly service with a personal touch.
  - Great for families and budget-conscious travelers seeking comfort and coziness.

5. Hotel Splendid Sole

Overview: Situated in Bardolino, this hotel combines modern amenities with traditional charm.

- Amenities:
  - Large outdoor pool surrounded by gardens.
  - Spa and wellness facilities, including a sauna and massage services.
  - Restaurant featuring local dishes and wines.

- Highlights:
  - Close proximity to the lake and local attractions.
  - Ideal for both families and couples seeking a relaxing vacation.

6. Hotel Ristorante Pizzeria La Rocca

Overview: Located in the picturesque town of Malcesine, this hotel offers stunning views of the lake and mountains.

- Amenities:
- Rooftop terrace and restaurant with panoramic views.
- Complimentary bikes and water sports equipment for guests.
- Family-friendly environment with spacious rooms.

- Highlights:
- A great base for exploring nearby hiking trails and the famous Monte Baldo cable car.
- Excellent dining options, including a renowned pizzeria.

7. Borgo degli Ulivi

Overview: This resort in the hills above Garda town features a blend of luxury and nature.

- Amenities:
- Infinity pool with breathtaking views over Lake Garda.
- Spa services and wellness programs.
- On-site restaurant focusing on organic and locally sourced ingredients.

- Highlights:
- Secluded location ideal for relaxation and nature lovers.
- Perfect for romantic getaways and wellness retreats.

Lake Garda offers a diverse selection of resorts and hotels that cater to every type of traveler. Whether you prefer the luxury of a five-star spa resort or the charm of a family-run boutique hotel, you'll find accommodations that enhance your experience in this beautiful region. Consider your preferences and activities when choosing where to stay, ensuring a memorable visit to Lake Garda.

3.2 Budget-Friendly Accommodations

If you're looking to enjoy Lake Garda without breaking the bank, there are plenty of budget-friendly accommodations that offer comfort and convenience. Here's a detailed guide to some of the best options for travelers on a budget.

1. Hostel Garda

Overview: Located in Desenzano del Garda, this hostel is perfect for backpackers and solo travelers.

- Amenities:
   - Dormitory-style and private rooms available.
   - Shared kitchen facilities for self-catering.
   - Common lounge area for socializing and relaxing.

- Highlights:
 - Affordable rates with a friendly atmosphere.
 - Close to the lakeside promenade and local attractions.

2. Hotel Villa Italia

Overview: Situated in Sirmione, this charming hotel offers comfortable rooms at reasonable prices.

- Amenities:
 - Free Wi-Fi and breakfast included.
 - Garden area with seating for guests.
 - Easy access to the lake and nearby thermal baths.

- Highlights:
 - Family-run establishment with personalized service.
 - Proximity to Sirmione's historic sites and beaches.

3. Camping La Rocca

Overview: For those who enjoy the outdoors, this campsite near Bardolino offers a unique experience.

- Amenities:
  - Tent and mobile home rentals available.
  - Swimming pools and sports facilities on-site.
  - Restaurant and grocery store for convenient dining options.

- Highlights:
  - Beautiful natural setting with direct access to the lake.
  - Great for families and groups looking for an adventurous stay.

4. Hotel Miralago

Overview: Located in Limone sul Garda, this hotel provides stunning views of the lake at budget-friendly prices.

- Amenities:
 - Basic but comfortable rooms, many with balconies.
 - On-site restaurant serving local cuisine.
 - Free parking and Wi-Fi.

- Highlights:
 - Charming atmosphere with a friendly staff.
 - Close to hiking paths and the lakeside promenade.

5. B&B La Vigna

Overview: This bed and breakfast in Bardolino offers a cozy stay with a personal touch.

- Amenities:
 - Simple, comfortable rooms with en-suite bathrooms.
 - Breakfast featuring local products.
 - Garden area for guests to relax in.

- Highlights:
 - Warm hospitality from the owners.

- Walking distance to the town center and lake.

6. Hotel Azzurra

Overview: Located in Peschiera del Garda, this hotel offers affordable accommodations close to the lake.

- Amenities:
  - Basic rooms with essential amenities.
  - On-site bar and outdoor terrace.
  - Free bicycle rentals for exploring the area.

- Highlights:
  - Convenient location near public transport and attractions.
  - Friendly atmosphere suitable for families and couples.

7. Ostello di Garda

Overview: This lakeside hostel in Garda town is perfect for budget-conscious travelers.

- Amenities:
   - Dormitory-style and private rooms available.

- Shared kitchen for self-catering.
- Outdoor terrace with lake views.

- Highlights:
- Vibrant community atmosphere with organized activities.
- Close proximity to local beaches and hiking trails.

Lake Garda has a wealth of budget-friendly accommodations that allow you to enjoy this beautiful region without overspending. From hostels and campsites to cozy B&Bs, there are options to suit every traveler's needs. By choosing budget-friendly lodging, you'll have more resources to explore the stunning landscapes, charming towns, and delicious cuisine that Lake Garda has to offer.

3.3 Unique Stays: Agriturismos and Villas

For a memorable experience at Lake Garda, consider staying at an agriturismo or a villa. These accommodations offer a unique blend of local culture, stunning scenery, and authentic Italian hospitality. Here's a detailed look at some of the best options.

1. Agriturismo Ca' dei Frati

Overview: Located near Salò, this agriturismo is set in a beautiful vineyard and olive grove.

- Amenities:
 - Comfortable rooms with rustic decor and private balconies.
 - On-site restaurant serving homemade meals made from local ingredients.
 - Wine tastings and tours of the vineyard available.

- Highlights:
 - Peaceful countryside setting with breathtaking views of Lake Garda.
 - Ideal for wine lovers and those seeking a tranquil retreat.

2. Agriturismo Le Fontanelle

Overview: Situated in the hills above Bardolino, this charming agriturismo offers a taste of rural life.

- Amenities:
  - Rustic rooms with modern comforts and en-suite bathrooms.
  - Outdoor swimming pool and sun terrace.
  - Farm-to-table meals featuring products from the property.

- Highlights:
  - Family-friendly atmosphere with activities for kids.
  - Close to hiking trails and cycling paths.

3. Villa Oliva

Overview: This luxurious villa located in Torri del Benaco combines elegance with stunning lake views.

- Amenities:
  - Spacious rooms with high-end furnishings and private terraces.

- Infinity pool overlooking the lake.
- Fully equipped kitchen for self-catering options.

- Highlights:
- Perfect for families or groups seeking privacy and comfort.
- Beautiful gardens and direct access to the lakeshore.

4. Agriturismo Corte Canai
Overview: Nestled in the countryside near Peschiera del Garda, this agriturismo offers a relaxing escape.

- Amenities:
- Cozy rooms with rustic charm and modern amenities.
- On-site farm with animals and vegetable gardens.
- Breakfast featuring homemade jams and local cheeses.

- Highlights:
- Ideal for families and nature lovers.

- Opportunities for outdoor activities like hiking and cycling.

5. Villa La Torre

Overview: Located in the scenic hills of Garda, this villa offers a luxurious stay with stunning views.

- Amenities:
   - Elegant rooms with classic decor and en-suite bathrooms.
   - Private pool and extensive gardens.
   - Close proximity to local attractions and the lake.

- Highlights:
   - A perfect choice for couples looking for a romantic getaway.
   - Great for those who appreciate history and architecture.

6. Agriturismo Al-Marnich

Overview: Perched in the mountains near Tremosine, this agriturismo offers breathtaking views and tranquility.

- Amenities:
  - Rustic rooms with wooden beams and country-style furnishings.
  - Restaurant serving traditional Italian dishes, many made from farm-fresh ingredients.
  - Hiking trails accessible from the property.

- Highlights:
  - Peaceful, secluded location ideal for nature enthusiasts.
  - Family-friendly with activities for children.

7. Villa dei Cedri

Overview: This historic villa in Lazise combines luxury with rich heritage.

- Amenities:
  - Classically styled rooms with luxurious amenities.
  - Large gardens, swimming pool, and wellness area.
  - On-site restaurant with a focus on local cuisine.

- Highlights:
   - Ideal for those seeking a blend of relaxation and cultural experiences.
   - Close to the lakeside and charming town of Lazise.

Staying at an agriturismo or villa around Lake Garda offers a unique opportunity to immerse yourself in the local culture and enjoy the region's stunning natural beauty. Whether you prefer the rustic charm of an agriturismo or the elegance of a villa, these accommodations provide a memorable experience that goes beyond typical hotel stays. Enjoy the tranquility, delicious local cuisine, and breathtaking views that make Lake Garda such a special destination.

Lake Garda Hotels

Scan to see all the hotels and places to stay at Lake Garda

- Boutique Hotel Villa Sostagazurro
- Hotel Du Lac
- Hotel Sirmione E Promessi Sposi
- Hotel Caesius Thermae & Spa Resort
- Hotel Caesius Thermae & Spa Resort

3.4 Camping by the Lake

Camping by Lake Garda is a fantastic way to connect with nature while enjoying the stunning scenery and vibrant outdoor activities the region has to offer. Here's a detailed guide to some of the best camping options around the lake.

1. Camping La Rocca

Overview: Located near Bardolino, Camping La Rocca is popular for its beautiful setting and family-friendly atmosphere.

- Amenities:

 - Spacious pitches for tents, camper vans, and caravans.

 - Swimming pools, playgrounds, and sports facilities.

 - Restaurant and bar on-site, plus a mini-market.

- Highlights:

 - Direct access to the lake and nearby beaches.

- Organized activities for children and adults, including sports and entertainment.

2. Camping Bella Italia
Overview: This large campsite in Peschiera del Garda offers a wide range of amenities and activities.

- Amenities:
- Various accommodation options, including mobile homes and glamping tents.
- Multiple swimming pools, water slides, and sports courts.
- Restaurants, shops, and entertainment programs.

- Highlights:
- Family-oriented with plenty of activities for all ages.
- Direct access to the lake and stunning views.

3. Camping Europa Silvella
Overview: Situated in San Felice del Benaco, this campsite is known for its natural beauty and tranquil environment.

- **Amenities:**
  - Pitches for tents and caravans, as well as rental bungalows.
  - Swimming pools, fitness area, and a beach bar.
  - On-site restaurant serving local cuisine.
- **Highlights:**
  - Nestled among olive trees with direct access to the shoreline.
  - Ideal for those seeking a peaceful retreat with opportunities for hiking and biking.

4. Camping San Francesco

Overview: Located in a scenic area in the town of Gargnano, Camping San Francesco is perfect for nature lovers.

- **Amenities:**
  - Well-equipped pitches for tents and caravans.
  - Swimming pool, beach access, and water sports rentals.
  - Restaurant and grocery store available on-site.
- **Highlights:**

- Breathtaking views of the lake and surrounding mountains.

- Great for outdoor activities like hiking, cycling, and water sports.

5. Camping Castello di Avio

Overview: This campsite is set in a picturesque location near the Avio Castle, offering a mix of history and nature.

- Amenities:

- Pitches for tents, camper vans, and caravans.

- Swimming pool, playground, and sports facilities.

- On-site dining options and a small shop.

- Highlights:

- Close to historical sites and hiking trails.

- A quieter alternative, ideal for couples and families.

6. Camping Internazionale

Overview: Located in Salò, this campsite combines comfort with a great location.

- Amenities:

- Pitches for tents and caravans, as well as mobile home rentals.

- Swimming pool, private beach access, and sports courts.

- Restaurant and bar with local dishes and drinks.

- Highlights:

- Convenient access to the town of Salò and local attractions.

- Family-friendly with organized activities.

7. Camping La Quercia

Overview: Situated in Lazise, this campsite is known for its extensive facilities and entertainment options.

- Amenities:

- Pitches and various rental accommodations available.

- Multiple swimming pools, wellness area, and sports activities.

- On-site restaurant, supermarket, and entertainment programs.

- Highlights:

- Ideal for families with children, offering numerous activities.
- Close to the lake and historic town of Lazise.

Camping by Lake Garda provides a unique and immersive way to enjoy the region's stunning landscapes and outdoor activities. With a variety of campsites offering different amenities and experiences, you can choose the perfect spot to relax, explore, and create lasting memories. Whether you prefer a lively family-friendly atmosphere or a peaceful retreat in nature, Lake Garda has something to offer every camper.

Chapter 4: Exploring the Towns of Lake Garda

4.1 Sirmione: History and Thermal Baths

Sirmione, a stunning peninsula jutting into Lake Garda, is renowned for its rich history, beautiful scenery, and therapeutic thermal baths. This charming town offers a perfect blend of cultural exploration and relaxation, making it a must-visit destination.

Historical Highlights

1. Scaliger Castle (Castello Scaligero)
- **Overview:** This medieval castle, dating back to the 13th century, is one of Sirmione's most iconic landmarks.
- **Features:**
  - Surrounded by a moat, the castle offers impressive views of the town and lake.
  - Visitors can explore the towers and walk along the fortress walls.

2. Grotte di Catullo
- **Overview:** The ruins of a Roman villa located at the tip of the peninsula, dating back to the 1st century AD.
- **Features:**
  - Offers stunning views of the lake and surrounding landscape.
  - The site includes ancient ruins, gardens, and a museum showcasing artifacts.

3. Historic Center
- **Overview:** Strolling through Sirmione's narrow, cobblestone streets is a delightful experience.

- **Highlights:**
  - Quaint shops, cafes, and gelaterias line the streets.
  - Historical buildings and charming piazzas create a picturesque atmosphere.

Thermal Baths

Sirmione is famous for its natural hot springs, attracting visitors seeking relaxation and wellness.

1. Terme di Sirmione

- **Overview:** A renowned spa complex that harnesses the therapeutic properties of the local thermal waters.
- **Features:**
  - Offers various treatments, including massages, mud therapies, and thermal baths.
  - Facilities include indoor and outdoor pools with panoramic views of the lake.

2. Aquaria Thermal Spa
- **Overview:** A luxurious spa located on the lakeshore, perfect for a day of pampering.
- **Amenities:**
   - Various wellness programs and spa treatments.
   - Relaxation areas with lake views, saunas, and steam rooms.

Local Cuisine

Sirmione boasts a variety of dining options, from traditional trattorias to upscale restaurants.
- **Specialties:**
   - Freshwater fish from Lake Garda, often grilled or served in local pasta dishes.
   - Local wines, particularly Lugana, which pairs beautifully with the region's cuisine.

Sirmione is a captivating destination that beautifully combines history and relaxation. Whether you're exploring ancient ruins, soaking in thermal baths, or savoring local dishes, this enchanting town offers a memorable experience for every traveler. A visit to Sirmione is not just a trip; it's an immersion into the rich culture and natural beauty of Lake Garda.

4.2 Desenzano del Garda: Vibrant Nightlife and Markets

Desenzano del Garda, located on the southern shore of Lake Garda, is known for its lively atmosphere, beautiful waterfront, and rich cultural offerings. This town is a fantastic destination for those seeking both relaxation during the day and vibrant nightlife after the sun sets.

Nightlife

Desenzano del Garda comes alive at night, with a variety of bars, clubs, and entertainment options catering to different tastes.

1. Bars and Pubs
- **Overview:** The town features numerous bars along the lakeshore and in the historic center, perfect for enjoying a drink with friends.
- **Popular Spots:**
  - **Bar Centrale:** Known for its cocktails and lively atmosphere, this bar is a favorite among locals and tourists alike.
  - **Cafè Cavour:** A charming café that transforms into a vibrant bar in the evening, offering live music and themed nights.

2. Clubs
- **Overview:** For those looking to dance the night away, Desenzano has several nightclubs that host DJ sets and live music.
- **Notable Clubs:**
  - **Alibi:** A popular nightclub known for its energetic vibe and diverse music selection, drawing a young crowd.
  - **Club 44:** Features themed nights and live performances, making it a great choice for a fun night out.

3. Live Music and Events
- **Overview:** Throughout the year, Desenzano hosts various music festivals and events that highlight local talent.
- **Highlights:**
  - **Summer Concert Series:** Held at various venues around town, featuring everything from jazz to pop.
  - **Cultural Events:** Check local listings for seasonal events that often include live performances, street parties, and more.

Markets
Desenzano del Garda is also known for its markets, offering a range of local products, crafts, and fresh produce.

1. Weekly Market
- **Overview:** Held every Tuesday morning in the historic center, this market is a must-visit for both locals and visitors.
- **What to Find:**
  - Fresh fruits, vegetables, and local cheeses.
  - Handmade crafts, clothing, and textiles.

- Local delicacies, including olive oil, wines, and pastries.

2. Flea Market

- **Overview:** Taking place on the first Sunday of each month, this flea market attracts treasure hunters and bargain seekers.
- **Highlights:**
  - Vintage items, antiques, and collectibles.
  - Unique souvenirs and handmade goods from local artisans.

3. Christmas Market

- **Overview:** During the holiday season, Desenzano hosts a charming Christmas market, perfect for festive shopping.
- **Features:**
  - Stalls adorned with lights selling holiday treats, crafts, and decorations.
  - Live music and entertainment, creating a magical atmosphere.

Dining Options

After enjoying the nightlife or shopping at the markets, Desenzano offers a variety of dining options.

- **Restaurants:**
  - **Ristorante La Gioconda:** Known for its fresh seafood and traditional Italian dishes, with a lovely lakeside view.
  - **Trattoria Da Rino:** A cozy spot famous for its homemade pasta and local wines.
- **Gelaterias:** Don't miss the chance to indulge in some of the best gelato in Italy, with numerous gelaterias scattered throughout the town.

Desenzano del Garda is a vibrant town that beautifully combines lively nightlife with charming local markets. Whether you're looking to dance the night away, enjoy a relaxing evening by the lake, or explore local crafts and delicacies, Desenzano offers a diverse array of experiences. This dynamic town is perfect for those seeking both adventure and relaxation in the stunning setting of Lake Garda.

4.3 Riva del Garda: Outdoor Adventures

Riva del Garda, located at the northern tip of Lake Garda, is a paradise for outdoor enthusiasts. Surrounded by dramatic mountains and crystal-clear waters, this town offers a wide range of activities for adventure seekers, from hiking and cycling to water sports and climbing. Here's a comprehensive guide to outdoor adventures in Riva del Garda.

Hiking and Trekking

1. Sentiero del Ponale
- **Overview:** This scenic trail offers breathtaking views of the lake and surrounding mountains.
- **Highlights:**
  - The path is suitable for all skill levels and follows an old road that was once used for transporting goods.
  - Expect stunning vistas of Lake Garda, especially from the viewpoints along the way.
- **Duration:** Approximately 1.5 to 2 hours one way.

2. Monte Baldo
- **Overview:** A mountain range offering various hiking trails with panoramic views.

- **Access:** Reachable via the cable car from Malcesine, making it accessible for hikers of all levels.
- **Highlights:**
  - Multiple trails to choose from, ranging from easy walks to challenging hikes.
  - The area is rich in flora and fauna, perfect for nature lovers.

3. Cascate di Varone
- **Overview:** A short hike to beautiful waterfalls located just outside Riva del Garda.
- **Features:**
  - A well-maintained path leads you through lush vegetation to the stunning falls.
  - Visitors can explore caves behind the waterfall for a unique perspective.

Cycling

1. Lake Garda Cycle Path
- **Overview:** A scenic cycling route that circles the lake, providing stunning views and a mix of terrains.
- **Highlights:**

- The path is mostly flat and suitable for cyclists of all levels.
   - Rent bikes from local shops in Riva del Garda for easy access to the trail.

2. Mountain Biking
- **Overview:** Riva del Garda is a hub for mountain biking enthusiasts, with numerous trails catering to different skill levels.
- **Popular Trails:**
   - **Tremalzo Pass:** A challenging route with stunning views, ideal for experienced bikers.
   - **Marmitte dei Giganti:** A moderate trail featuring unique geological formations.

Water Sports

1. Sailing and Windsurfing
- **Overview:** The consistent winds and calm waters make Riva del Garda a popular spot for sailing and windsurfing.

- **Rental Options:** Various local schools and rental shops offer equipment and lessons for beginners and experienced sailors alike.

2. Kayaking and Stand-Up Paddleboarding
- **Overview:** Explore the lake at your own pace with kayaking or paddleboarding.
- **Rental Services:** Equipment is readily available from local shops, and guided tours can be arranged for a more structured experience.

Climbing and Bouldering

1. Via Ferrata
- **Overview:** Riva del Garda is home to several via ferrata routes, providing thrilling climbing experiences for adventurers.
- **Popular Routes:**
    - **Via Ferrata del Colodri:** Offers stunning views and is suitable for those with some climbing experience.

- **Via Ferrata Cima SAT:** A more challenging route with incredible vistas of the surrounding landscape.

2. Bouldering
- **Overview:** The area around Riva del Garda features numerous bouldering spots for climbing enthusiasts.
- **Locations:** Local climbing gyms and outdoor bouldering areas provide options for climbers of all levels.

Riva del Garda is an outdoor adventure haven, offering something for everyone. Whether you prefer hiking through stunning landscapes, cycling along scenic paths, or engaging in thrilling water sports, this town provides a perfect backdrop for your adventures. With its combination of natural beauty and diverse activities, Riva del Garda is a must-visit destination for any outdoor enthusiast exploring Lake Garda.

4.4 Malcesine: Cable Cars and Castles

Malcesine, a charming town on the eastern shore of Lake Garda, is known for its stunning landscapes, historic castle, and the breathtaking cable car that ascends to Monte Baldo. This picturesque destination offers a perfect blend of history, adventure, and natural beauty.

Castles
1. Castello Scaligero
- **Overview:** This medieval castle, perched atop a rocky promontory, is one of Malcesine's most iconic landmarks.
- **History:**
  - Originally built in the 6th century, it has been expanded and renovated over the centuries.
  - The castle served as a fortress and residence for the noble Scaliger family.

- **Features:**
  - Explore the castle's towers, walls, and courtyard for stunning views of the lake and surrounding mountains.
  - The castle houses a small museum showcasing historical artifacts and exhibits related to the region's history.
- **Highlights:**
  - The panoramic views from the top of the castle are spectacular, providing a perfect photo opportunity.

- The surrounding gardens are a peaceful place to relax and enjoy the scenery.

Cable Cars
1. Monte Baldo Cable Car
- **Overview:** The cable car from Malcesine to Monte Baldo offers a thrilling ride with spectacular views of Lake Garda and the surrounding mountains.
- **Experience:**
   - The ride takes about 10 minutes, ascending over 1,700 meters.
   - The cable car features rotating cabins, allowing passengers to enjoy 360-degree views during the ascent.
- **Activities at Monte Baldo:**
   - **Hiking:** Once at the top, a network of trails awaits, ranging from easy walks to challenging hikes.
   - **Mountain Biking:** The area is popular for downhill mountain biking, with trails catering to different skill levels.
   - **Paragliding:** For the adventurous, paragliding offers an exhilarating way to

experience the stunning landscapes from above.

2. Dining and Relaxation

- **Restaurants:** Enjoy a meal at one of the mountain restaurants serving local cuisine, with stunning views as your backdrop.
- **Picnic Spots:** Bring a picnic to enjoy in the beautiful alpine meadows, surrounded by nature.

Local Life and Culture

1. Historic Center

- **Overview:** Malcesine's historic center features narrow cobblestone streets, charming shops, and cafes.

- **Highlights:**
  - Visit local boutiques for unique souvenirs and artisan products.
  - Enjoy a coffee or gelato at a lakeside café while soaking in the vibrant atmosphere.

2. Events and Festivals

- **Overview:** Malcesine hosts various cultural events throughout the year, including:
  - **Festa di San Marco:** Celebrated in April, featuring processions, music, and local traditions.
  - **Lake Garda Wine Festival:** Showcasing local wines and culinary delights, typically held in the summer.

Malcesine is a delightful destination that beautifully combines history and adventure. From exploring the majestic Castello

Scaligero to riding the cable car up to Monte Baldo, visitors can immerse themselves in the rich culture and stunning landscapes of Lake Garda. Whether you're seeking outdoor activities or a taste of local heritage, Malcesine offers something for everyone, making it a must-visit town on your journey around the lake.

4.5 Bardolino: Wine Country and Lakeside Beauty

Bardolino, nestled along the eastern shore of Lake Garda, is renowned for its picturesque landscapes, charming streets, and, most notably, its wine production. This delightful town is a perfect destination for those looking to experience both the natural beauty of the lake and the rich viticultural heritage of the region.

Wine Country

1. Bardolino Wine

- **Overview:** Bardolino is famous for its red wines, particularly the Bardolino DOC and the Bardolino Superiore DOCG.
- **Characteristics:**
  - **Bardolino DOC:** Typically light and fruity, made primarily from Corvina, Rondinella, and Molinara grapes.
  - **Bardolino Superiore DOCG:** A more refined version, aged longer and offering deeper flavors.

2. Wine Tours and Tastings

- **Overview:** The surrounding countryside is dotted with vineyards and wineries, many of which offer tours and tastings.
- **Popular Wineries:**
  - **Cantina Zeni:** Features a museum dedicated to wine production and offers tastings in a beautiful setting.
  - **Azienda Agricola Ca' dei Frati:** Known for its stunning views and excellent wine selection.

- **Experiences:**
  - Guided tours through vineyards, explaining the winemaking process.
  - Pairing local wines with traditional Italian dishes, enhancing the culinary experience.

Lakeside Beauty
1. Lakeside Promenade
- **Overview:** Bardolino boasts a scenic lakeside promenade perfect for leisurely strolls or cycling.
- **Features:**
  - Lined with palm trees, gardens, and charming cafes, the promenade offers stunning views of Lake Garda.
  - Benches and picnic areas provide opportunities to relax and enjoy the serene environment.

2. Beaches
- **Overview:** The town has several public beaches that are ideal for sunbathing and swimming.

- **Popular Spots:**
  - **Spiaggia Mirabello:** A family-friendly beach with shallow waters and amenities.
  - **Spiaggia Punta Cornicello:** A quieter spot, perfect for a peaceful day by the lake.

Local Culture and Activities

1. Historic Center

- **Overview:** Bardolino's historic center features charming streets, quaint shops, and vibrant piazzas.

- **Highlights:**
  - Visit the Church of San Zeno, known for its beautiful frescoes and historical significance.
  - Explore local artisan shops for unique souvenirs, including handmade crafts and local delicacies.

2. Festivals and Events

- **Overview:** Bardolino hosts several festivals celebrating its wine culture and local traditions.

- **Key Events:**
  - **Bardolino Wine Festival:** Held in October, featuring tastings, food stalls, and live music.
  - **Sagra dell'Uva:** A grape festival celebrating the harvest with parades, music, and local food.

Culinary Delights

- **Restaurants:** Bardolino offers a range of dining options, from casual trattorias to upscale restaurants.
- **Specialties:**
  - **Local Fish Dishes:** Freshwater fish from Lake Garda, often grilled and served with local olive oil.
  - **Pasta and Risotto:** Made with seasonal ingredients, showcasing the flavors of the region.

Chapter 5: Top Attractions and Things to Do

5.1 Boat Tours and Lake Excursions

Exploring Lake Garda by boat is one of the most enchanting ways to experience this stunning region of Italy. With its picturesque towns, dramatic cliffs, and crystal-clear waters, a boat tour offers a unique perspective on the lake's beauty. Here's a detailed guide to the various boat tours and excursions available on Lake Garda.

Types of Boat Tours

1. **Public Ferries**
- **Overview:** The public ferry system connects major towns around Lake Garda, making it easy to explore multiple destinations in one day.

- **Key Routes:**
  - **Desenzano to Riva del Garda:** A scenic journey that showcases the lake's stunning vistas.
  - **Bardolino to Limone:** A picturesque route that takes you past charming villages and lush landscapes.
- **Experience:** Ferries run frequently and offer both indoor and outdoor seating, allowing passengers to enjoy the fresh lake breeze and stunning views.

2. Private Boat Rentals

- **Overview:** For those seeking a more personalized experience, renting a boat is a fantastic option.
- **Options:**
  - **Motorboats:** Perfect for families or groups wanting to explore at their own pace.
  - **Sailboats:** Ideal for sailing enthusiasts or those wishing to learn.
- **Experience:** Many rental companies provide guidance and equipment, making it accessible even for beginners. Enjoy a picnic

on the water or anchor at a secluded cove for swimming.

3. Guided Boat Tours
- **Overview:** These tours are led by knowledgeable guides who share insights about the lake's history, culture, and natural beauty.
- **Types of Tours:**
  - **Historical Tours:** Focus on the rich history of the towns along the lake, including visits to ancient sites and landmarks.
  - **Wine and Dine Tours:** Combine scenic views with wine tastings and gourmet meals at lakeside restaurants.
- **Highlights:**
  - **Limone sul Garda:** Known for its lemon groves and vibrant architecture.
  - **Sirmione:** Famous for its thermal baths and the stunning Scaliger Castle.

Popular Excursions
1. The Sirmione Peninsula
- **Overview:** A must-see destination, known for its stunning landscapes and historical sites.
- **Activities:**
  - **Visit Scaliger Castle:** Explore this medieval fortress with panoramic views of the lake.
  - **Relax in the Thermal Baths:** Enjoy spa treatments utilizing the natural hot springs.

2. Isola del Garda
- **Overview:** The largest island on Lake Garda, famous for its lush gardens and historic villa.
- **Experience:**
  - Guided tours of the villa and gardens, showcasing stunning architecture and exotic plants.

- Opportunities for swimming and relaxing in the tranquil surroundings.

3. The Northern Shores
- **Overview:** Explore the more rugged and scenic northern part of the lake.
- **Highlights:**
  - **Riva del Garda:** Known for its outdoor activities and beautiful waterfront.
  - **Tremosine:** Famous for its breathtaking cliffside views and the scenic Strada della Forra.

Sunset Cruises

- **Overview:** Experience the magic of Lake Garda at sunset with a dedicated evening cruise.
- **Highlights:**
    - Enjoy a romantic atmosphere with beautiful views as the sun sets over the mountains.
    - Many cruises offer dinner options, allowing you to dine while taking in the stunning scenery.

Tips for Boat Tours

- **Booking in Advance:** Especially during peak season, it's advisable to book tours or rentals in advance to secure your spot.
- **What to Bring:** Sunscreen, hats, and water are essential, along with a camera to capture the stunning views.
- **Dress Code:** Casual and comfortable clothing is recommended, with layers for cooler evenings.

Boat tours and lake excursions are among the best ways to experience the breathtaking beauty of Lake Garda. Whether you choose a public ferry, a private rental, or a guided tour, you'll create unforgettable memories as you explore the enchanting towns and stunning landscapes surrounding this magnificent lake. Embrace the serenity of the water and the charm of the lakeside villages for an enriching experience in this Italian paradise.

5.2 Visiting Castles: Scaliger Castle and More

Lake Garda is not only known for its stunning landscapes but also for its rich history, prominently featured in its magnificent castles. Among these, Scaliger Castle stands out as a must-visit attraction, but there are several other historical sites worth exploring. Here's a detailed guide to the castles around Lake Garda.

Scaliger Castle (Castello Scaligero)

Overview
- **Location:** Sirmione, on the southern tip of Lake Garda.
- **History:** Built in the 13th century by the Scaliger family, it served as a fortress to protect the region.

Architectural Features

- **Design:** The castle features impressive battlements, towers, and a drawbridge, showcasing medieval military architecture.
- **Interior:** Explore the well-preserved courtyard, towers, and living quarters, which provide a glimpse into the life of nobility during the medieval period.

Highlights
- **Panoramic Views:** Climb to the top of the castle for breathtaking views of Lake Garda and the surrounding landscape.

- **Museum:** The castle houses a small museum with exhibits on local history and artifacts.

Visitor Information
- **Opening Hours:** Typically open year-round, but hours may vary by season.
- **Admission Fee:** A small fee is usually charged for entry.

Other Notable Castles Around Lake Garda

1. Castello di Malcesine
- **Overview:** A striking castle located in Malcesine, overlooking the lake.
- **History:** Originally built in the 5th century, it was expanded in the 14th century by the Scaliger family.

Features
- **Architecture:** A mix of Roman and medieval styles, with a picturesque tower that dominates the skyline.

- **Museum:** The castle includes a museum dedicated to the history of the area and the natural environment.

Highlights
- **Breathtaking Views:** Like Scaliger Castle, it offers stunning views of Lake Garda from its ramparts.
- **Access:** Easily reachable from the town center, making it a convenient stop for visitors.

2. Castello di Arco
- **Overview:** Located just north of Riva del Garda, this castle is perched on a hilltop.
- **History:** Dates back to the 11th century, it served as a strategic military site.

Features
- **Ruins:** The castle is mostly in ruins, but the remnants tell a story of its past glory.
- **Gardens:** The surrounding area is filled with lush gardens and hiking trails.

Highlights
- **Hiking:** A popular hiking destination, offering scenic trails leading to the castle.
- **Viewpoint:** Provides spectacular views of the Sarca Valley and Lake Garda.

3. Castello di Soiano
- **Overview:** A lesser-known but charming castle located in Soiano del Lago.
- **History:** Built in the 11th century, it served as a lookout point.

Features
- **Ruins and Walls:** While in ruins, the castle walls and towers remain impressive.
- **Historic Significance:** Offers insights into the region's medieval past.

Highlights
- **Peaceful Atmosphere:** Less crowded than other castles, making it a peaceful spot to explore.

- **Surrounding Nature:** Surrounded by vineyards and olive groves, perfect for a leisurely walk.

Tips for Visiting Castles

- **Plan Your Visits:** Check opening hours and any special events or guided tours available.
- **Dress Comfortably:** Wear comfortable shoes for exploring uneven terrain and climbing stairs.
- **Photography:** Bring a camera to capture the stunning views and architectural details.
- **Combine Visits:** Consider combining visits to nearby castles for a full day of exploration.

Exploring the castles around Lake Garda offers a fascinating glimpse into the region's rich history and stunning architecture. From the iconic Scaliger Castle in Sirmione to the lesser-known gems like Castello di Soiano, each castle provides a unique experience and breathtaking views. Whether you're a history buff or simply looking to enjoy picturesque landscapes, these castles are essential stops on your Lake Garda itinerary.

5.3 Nature and Parks: Parco Alto Garda Bresciano

Overview

Parco Alto Garda Bresciano is a stunning natural park located in the northern part of Lake Garda, straddling the border between Lombardy and Trentino. This expansive area is known for its breathtaking landscapes, diverse flora and fauna, and numerous outdoor activities, making it a favorite destination for nature lovers and adventure seekers.

Key Features

1. Diverse Ecosystems
- **Flora:** The park is home to a variety of plant species, including Mediterranean scrub, oak forests, and lush meadows. The

unique microclimates create a rich biodiversity.
- **Fauna:** Visitors may encounter various wildlife, including deer, foxes, and numerous bird species, making it a prime spot for birdwatching.

2. Stunning Landscapes
- **Scenic Views:** The park offers breathtaking vistas of Lake Garda and the surrounding mountains. Numerous viewpoints provide perfect photo opportunities.
- **Geological Features:** Explore rugged cliffs, rolling hills, and deep valleys that showcase the area's geological diversity.

Outdoor Activities
1. Hiking
- **Trails:** The park boasts a network of well-marked hiking trails suitable for all skill levels. Routes range from easy walks to more challenging hikes that lead to panoramic viewpoints.

- **Popular Trails:**
  - **Sentiero del Ventrar:** A scenic trail that offers stunning views of the lake and surrounding mountains.
  - **Sentiero dei Piani di Spino:** A moderate hike that takes you through picturesque forests and meadows.

2. Mountain Biking
- **Overview:** The park features various mountain biking trails, catering to both beginners and experienced riders.
- **Trail Highlights:** Routes often pass through vineyards, olive groves, and charming villages, providing a unique way to experience the landscape.

3. Water Activities
- **Kayaking and Canoeing:** The clear waters of Lake Garda are perfect for kayaking and canoeing, allowing you to explore the beautiful shoreline and hidden coves.

- **Fishing:** Anglers can enjoy fishing in designated areas, with opportunities to catch various freshwater species.

Visitor Information
1. Access Points
- **Main Entrances:** The park can be accessed from several towns, including Gargnano, Salò, and Tignale, each offering different entry points and facilities.

2. Facilities
- **Visitor Centers:** Several visitor centers provide information on park activities, maps, and guided tours.
- **Rest Areas:** Picnic areas and rest spots are available throughout the park, making it easy to relax and enjoy the scenery.

3. Guided Tours
- **Overview:** For those wishing to learn more about the park's natural history and ecology, guided tours are available. These

tours often include hiking, wildlife spotting, and educational talks.

5.4 Amusement Parks: Gardaland and Caneva World

Lake Garda is not only renowned for its natural beauty and historical sites but also for its thrilling amusement parks. Two of the most popular parks in the region are Gardaland and Caneva World, offering a perfect blend of excitement and entertainment for visitors of all ages.

Gardaland
Overview
- **Location:** Situated near Peschiera del Garda, Gardaland is one of Italy's largest and most famous amusement parks.
- **Established:** Opened in 1975, it has since become a top attraction for families and thrill-seekers.

Attractions
1. Roller Coasters
- **Raptor:** A thrilling winged coaster that offers an exhilarating ride with multiple inversions and high speeds.
- **Blue Tornado:** A classic indoor coaster featuring spirals and sudden drops that will test your nerves.

2. Family Rides

- **Pirates' Island:** An immersive family-friendly ride that takes you through a pirate-themed adventure.

- **Jungle Rapids:** A water ride that combines splashes and excitement, perfect for cooling off on warm days.

3. Live Shows and Entertainment

- **Themed Shows:** Throughout the day, visitors can enjoy live performances, including magic shows, acrobatics, and musical acts.

- **Character Meet-and-Greets:** Opportunities to meet beloved characters from popular children's shows.

Visitor Information

- **Opening Hours:** Varies by season, typically open from late spring to early autumn.

- **Tickets:** Various ticket options are available, including single-day and multi-day passes.

Caneva World

Overview

- **Location:** Located in Lazise, just a short drive from Gardaland, Caneva World is a water park and amusement park combined.

- **Established:** Opened in the 1980s, it has evolved into a popular destination for fun and relaxation.

Attractions

1. Water Park

- **Aquapark:** Features numerous slides, wave pools, and lazy rivers, catering to all ages.

- **Kamikaze:** A high-speed slide that promises an adrenaline rush for thrill-seekers.

2. Amusement Rides

- **Themed Rides:** Enjoy attractions based on popular movies and themes, such as the Hollywood Action Tower, offering a thrilling drop experience.

- **Family Rides:** Various gentle rides suitable for younger children and families, ensuring everyone can join in the fun.

3. Live Entertainment

- **Stunt Shows:** Spectacular live shows feature stunts, pyrotechnics, and water tricks, captivating audiences of all ages.

Visitor Information

- **Opening Hours:** Generally operates from late spring through summer, with specific hours depending on the season.
- **Tickets:** Combination tickets for both the water park and amusement rides are available, providing excellent value for families.

Tips for Visiting

- **Plan Ahead:** Check the official websites for the latest information on opening hours, ticket prices, and any special events.
- **Arrive Early:** To make the most of your day, arrive early to avoid long lines for popular rides.

- **Stay Hydrated:** Especially during the summer months, stay hydrated and take breaks in shaded areas.
- **Wear Comfortable Shoes:** Expect a lot of walking, so wear comfortable footwear.

Chapter 6: Best Hikes and Outdoor Activities

6.1 Hiking Trails Around Lake Garda

Lake Garda is a hiker's paradise, offering a diverse range of trails that cater to all skill levels. From scenic lakeside paths to challenging mountain hikes, the area is rich in natural beauty and breathtaking views. Here's a guide to some of the best hiking trails around Lake Garda.

1. Sentiero del Ventrar
- **Location:** Gargnano
- **Difficulty:** Moderate
- **Distance:** Approximately 10 km (6.2 miles)
- **Highlights:**
  - This trail offers stunning views of Lake Garda as it winds through olive groves and Mediterranean vegetation.

- Look out for the ancient stone walls and charming rural landscapes.

2. Sentiero dei Piani di Spino
- **Location:** Tremosine
- **Difficulty:** Moderate to Challenging
- **Distance:** About 14 km (8.7 miles)
- **Highlights:**
  - The trail leads to the Piani di Spino plateau, providing panoramic views of the lake and surrounding mountains.
  - Ideal for photography enthusiasts, especially at sunrise and sunset.

3. Monte Baldo
- **Location:** Malcesine
- **Difficulty:** Varies (multiple trails)
- **Distance:** Varies (up to 20 km/12.4 miles)
- **Highlights:**
  - Accessible via a cable car, Monte Baldo offers several trails ranging from easy walks to challenging hikes.

- Enjoy breathtaking views of the entire lake and the Alps.

4. Sentiero della Ponale
- **Location:** Riva del Garda
- **Difficulty:** Easy to Moderate
- **Distance:** Approximately 10 km (6.2 miles) round trip
- **Highlights:**
  - A historic path along the cliffs, featuring views of the lake and stunning rock formations.
  - Suitable for families and offers a glimpse into the region's history.

5. Sentiero del Garda
- **Location:** Various starting points around the lake
- **Difficulty:** Moderate
- **Distance:** Approximately 40 km (24.9 miles) (can be done in sections)
- **Highlights:**

- This long-distance trail runs along the western shore of Lake Garda, connecting several towns.
   - Features diverse landscapes, including beaches, forests, and charming villages.

6. Cima Capi
   - **Location:** Near Riva del Garda
   - **Difficulty:** Moderate
   - **Distance:** About 8 km (5 miles) round trip
   - **Highlights:**
     - This trail leads to the Cima Capi peak, where visitors can explore historic military ruins from World War I.
     - Offers spectacular views over Lake Garda and surrounding mountains.

Tips for Hiking Around Lake Garda
   - **Check Weather Conditions:** Always check the weather forecast before heading out, as conditions can change rapidly in the mountains.

- **Pack Essentials:** Bring water, snacks, a map, and sun protection. Good hiking shoes are essential for uneven terrain.
- **Respect Nature:** Stick to marked trails and pack out any trash to help preserve the natural beauty of the area.
- **Local Guides:** Consider hiring a local guide for more challenging hikes to enhance your experience and safety.

The hiking trails around Lake Garda offer something for everyone, whether you're an experienced hiker or a casual walker. With stunning views, diverse landscapes, and rich history, these trails provide an unforgettable way to experience the beauty of the region. Lace up your hiking boots and explore the natural wonders that Lake Garda has to offer!

6.2 Cycling Routes and Bike Rentals

Lake Garda is an ideal destination for cycling enthusiasts, offering a mix of scenic routes, challenging terrains, and breathtaking views. Whether you're looking for leisurely lakeside paths or adventurous mountain trails, there's something for every cyclist. Here's a guide to the best cycling routes and bike rental options in the area.

Popular Cycling Routes
1. Lake Garda Circuit

- **Distance:** Approximately 140 km (87 miles)
- **Difficulty:** Moderate
- **Route Highlights:**
  - A full circuit around the lake that takes you through charming towns like Peschiera del Garda, Sirmione, and Riva del Garda.

- Enjoy stunning views of the lake, vineyards, and olive groves along the way.

2. Mincio River Path

  - **Distance:** About 43 km (27 miles)
  - **Difficulty:** Easy
  - **Route Highlights:**
  - This flat, well-maintained path runs from Peschiera del Garda to Mantova, following the Mincio River.
  - Ideal for families, with beautiful landscapes and opportunities for picnicking.

3. Tremosine Loop

  - **Distance:** Approximately 25 km (15.5 miles)
  - **Difficulty:** Moderate to Challenging
  - **Route Highlights:**
  - A hilly route with breathtaking views of Lake Garda from high vantage points.
  - Explore the picturesque village of Tremosine and its famous scenic roads.

4. Valle dei Mulini

- **Distance:** About 10 km (6.2 miles)
- **Difficulty:** Moderate
- **Route Highlights:**
  - A scenic ride through the valley featuring old water mills and lush landscapes.
  - Great for those looking to explore nature and local history.

Bike Rentals

1. Local Bike Shops

- **Overview:** Numerous bike rental shops are available in towns around Lake Garda, offering a range of bicycles from mountain bikes to electric bikes.
- **Popular Rentals:**
  - **Bici Garda:** Located in Riva del Garda, offering high-quality bikes and guided tours.

- **Bike Rental Garda:** Based in Bardolino, with a variety of bikes and accessories for rent.

2. Rental Services

- **Online Reservations:** Many rental shops allow online booking, making it easy to secure your bike in advance.
- **Delivery Services:** Some companies offer delivery to your accommodation, providing convenience for travelers.

Tips for Cycling Around Lake Garda

- **Safety First:** Wear a helmet, use bike lights, and follow local traffic rules. Some routes may have steep sections, so be cautious.
- **Hydration and Snacks:** Carry water and snacks, especially on longer rides. There are many scenic spots to take breaks.

- **Check the Weather:** Be aware of weather conditions, as they can change quickly in mountainous areas.
- **Explore Off the Beaten Path:** Don't hesitate to venture into smaller trails and roads for unique views and experiences.

Cycling around Lake Garda offers an exhilarating way to explore the region's natural beauty and charming towns. With a variety of well-marked routes and convenient bike rental options, it's easy to enjoy a day of adventure on two wheels. Whether you're a casual rider or a seasoned cyclist, the stunning landscapes and fresh air await you!

6.3 Windsurfing, Sailing, and Water Sports

Lake Garda, with its stunning scenery and favorable winds, is a premier destination for water sports enthusiasts. From windsurfing to sailing, the lake offers a variety of activities that cater to both beginners and experienced athletes. Here's a guide to the best water sports options available around Lake Garda.

Windsurfing

Overview

- **Ideal Locations:** The northern part of Lake Garda, particularly in areas like Torbole and Riva del Garda, is known for its consistent winds, making it a hotspot for windsurfing.

- **Conditions:** The lake experiences two main winds: the Pelèr (morning wind) and the Ora (afternoon wind), providing excellent conditions throughout the day.

Rental and Lessons

- **Windsurfing Schools:** Various schools offer lessons for all skill levels, including:

   - **Surf Segnana (Torbole):** Offers rentals, lessons, and guided tours.

- **Wind's Up (Riva del Garda):** Provides instruction and equipment rental, focusing on safety and skill development.

Sailing
Overview
- **Sailing Conditions:** Lake Garda is known for its reliable wind patterns, making it a perfect location for both leisurely sailing and competitive racing.
- **Scenic Views:** Sailors can enjoy breathtaking vistas of the surrounding mountains and charming lakeside towns.

Rental and Lessons
- **Sailing Schools:** Many schools and clubs offer sailing lessons and equipment rentals:
  - **Circolo Vela Torbole:** Offers sailing courses and boat rentals, catering to all experience levels.
  - **Sailing Club Riva:** Provides lessons and the opportunity to rent sailboats, including dinghies and larger yachts.

Other Water Sports

1. Kayaking and Canoeing
- **Overview:** Kayaking is a popular way to explore the shoreline and hidden coves of Lake Garda.
- **Rental Options:** Many rental shops in towns like Malcesine and Limone offer kayaks and canoes for hire.

2. Stand-Up Paddleboarding (SUP)
- **Overview:** SUP is an increasingly popular activity on Lake Garda, providing a fun way to enjoy the water while getting a workout.
- **Rental Locations:** Various shops offer paddleboard rentals, and many provide lessons for beginners.

3. Jet Skiing
- **Overview:** For those seeking thrills, jet skiing is available in designated areas around the lake.
- **Rental Services:** Several companies offer jet ski rentals along with guided tours for a unique experience.

Tips for Water Sports at Lake Garda

- **Safety Gear:** Always wear a life jacket and follow safety guidelines provided by rental shops and instructors.

- **Weather Awareness:** Monitor weather conditions and wind patterns, especially if you're inexperienced.

- **Respect Local Regulations:** Stay within designated areas for water sports to ensure safety and protect local wildlife.

Lake Garda is a haven for water sports enthusiasts, offering a range of activities from windsurfing to sailing and beyond. With stunning landscapes and favorable conditions, it's the perfect place to enjoy an adventurous day on the water. Whether you're a seasoned pro or just starting out, the lake's vibrant water sports scene awaits!

6.4 Rock Climbing and Adventure Parks

Lake Garda is not only renowned for its beautiful lake and picturesque towns but also for its thrilling outdoor activities, including rock climbing and adventure parks. These pursuits offer adrenaline-pumping experiences for adventurers of all skill levels.

Rock Climbing
Overview
- **Climbing Areas:** The region boasts numerous climbing spots, with routes suitable for both beginners and seasoned climbers.
- **Scenic Backdrops:** Climbers can enjoy breathtaking views of Lake Garda and the surrounding mountains.

Popular Climbing Locations

1. Torbole
- **Characteristics:** Known for its limestone cliffs, offering a variety of sport climbing routes.
- **Highlights:** The crag is easily accessible and features routes of various difficulties.

2. Riva del Garda
- **Characteristics:** Offers both sport climbing and multi-pitch routes.
- **Highlights:** The views from the climbing routes are spectacular, overlooking the lake.

3. Arco
- **Characteristics:** Famous for its extensive climbing options, including traditional and sport routes.
- **Highlights:** Hosts numerous climbing competitions and festivals, making it a hub for climbers.

Climbing Schools and Guides

- **Guided Climbing:** Various local companies offer guided climbing experiences, ensuring safety and providing expert instruction.
- **Example:** Arco Climbing School provides courses for all levels, focusing on technique and safety.

Adventure Park

Overview

- **Family-Friendly Fun:** Adventure parks around Lake Garda offer tree-top courses, zip lines, and obstacle courses, making them perfect for families and groups.
- **Nature Immersion:** These parks are set in beautiful natural surroundings, allowing visitors to enjoy the outdoors.

Notable Adventure Parks

1. Busatte Adventure Park
- **Location:** Near Torbole

- **Features:** Includes various climbing routes, zip lines, and aerial courses set high among the trees.

- **Suitable For:** All ages, with courses designed for different skill levels.

2. Adventure Park Garda
- **Location:** Near Salò
- **Features:** Offers a variety of trails suspended between trees, including zip lines and climbing challenges.
- **Activities:** Perfect for a fun day out, with options for both kids and adults.

3. Forest Park
- **Location:** Near Desenzano del Garda
- **Features:** A large park with numerous treetop courses, zip lines, and a focus on safety.
- **Suitable For:** Families looking for adventure in a natural setting.

Tips for Rock Climbing and Adventure Parks

- **Safety First:** Always use proper safety equipment and follow guidelines provided by instructors.
- **Book in Advance:** For guided climbing or visits to popular adventure parks, consider booking ahead, especially during peak seasons.
- **Wear Appropriate Gear:** Comfortable clothing and footwear are essential, especially for climbing and navigating obstacle courses.
- **Hydrate and Snack:** Bring water and snacks, as outdoor activities can be physically demanding.

Rock climbing and adventure parks around Lake Garda offer exhilarating experiences for those seeking adventure in stunning natural settings. Whether you're scaling cliffs or navigating treetop courses, the region provides ample opportunities for outdoor fun and exploration, making it a must-visit for adventure enthusiasts!

Chapter 7: Guided Tours and Local Experiences

7.1 Wine Tasting and Vineyard Tours

Lake Garda is not only famous for its stunning landscapes but also for its rich wine culture. The region boasts a variety of vineyards and wineries that produce exceptional wines, making it a perfect destination for wine lovers. Here's a guide to the best wine tasting experiences and vineyard tours around Lake Garda.

Popular Wine Regions
1. Valpolicella
- **Overview:** Located just east of Lake Garda, Valpolicella is renowned for its Amarone and Valpolicella wines.
- **Wineries to Visit:**
   - **Allegrini:** Known for its high-quality Amarone, offering guided tours and tastings.

- **Tommasi Viticoltori:** Offers a comprehensive tour of the vineyard and cellar, with tastings of their renowned wines.

2. Bardolino
- **Overview:** Situated on the eastern shore of Lake Garda, Bardolino is famous for its light red wines.
- **Wineries to Visit:**
   - **Azienda Agricola Le Fraghe:** A family-run winery providing tastings and a tour of their beautiful vineyards.
   - **Corte Gardoni:** Known for its Bardolino and Chiaretto wines, offering tastings in a charming setting.

3. Garda Classico
- **Overview:** This region produces a variety of white, red, and rosé wines, with unique local varieties.
- **Wineries to Visit:**
   - **Cascina Maddalena:** Offers personalized tours and tastings, focusing on organic wine production.

- **Azienda Agricola Scolari:** Known for its traditional methods and a welcoming tasting experience.

Wine Tasting Experiences
1. Guided Tours
- **Overview:** Many wineries offer guided tours that include a walk through the vineyards, a look at the winemaking process, and tastings of various wines.
- **What to Expect:**
   - Insight into local grape varieties and winemaking techniques.
   - The opportunity to taste wines paired with local cheeses and cured meats.

2. Wine and Food Pairing
- **Overview:** Some wineries provide experiences that combine wine tasting with local culinary delights.
- **Highlights:**
  - Enjoying a multi-course meal paired with specific wines from the vineyard.

- Cooking classes that incorporate local ingredients and wines.

Tips for Wine Tasting and Vineyard Tours

- **Book in Advance:** Popular wineries can fill up quickly, especially during peak tourist seasons. Reservations are recommended.
- **Know Your Preferences:** Familiarize yourself with the types of wines you enjoy to enhance your tasting experience.
- **Transportation:** Consider arranging transport or a designated driver if you plan to visit multiple wineries.
- **Respect the Experience:** Be open to trying new wines and ask questions to learn more about the region's winemaking heritage.

Wine tasting and vineyard tours around Lake Garda offer a delightful way to experience the region's rich culture and culinary traditions. With beautiful landscapes, exceptional wines, and knowledgeable hosts, these experiences are sure to create lasting memories for any wine enthusiast. Whether you're a novice or a connoisseur, Lake Garda's wine country has something special in store for you!

7.2 Guided Historical Tours and Day Trips

Lake Garda is steeped in history, with its charming towns, ancient ruins, and beautiful castles. Guided historical tours and day trips provide an enriching way to explore the region's cultural heritage. Here's a guide to some of the best options available.

Historical Tours

1. Sirmione

- **Overview:** Sirmione is famous for its medieval castle, the Scaligero Castle, and the ancient Roman villa, Grotte di Catullo.
- **Tour Highlights:**

- **Scaligero Castle:** Explore this well-preserved fortress with stunning views of the lake.
- **Grotte di Catullo:** Visit the ruins of a Roman villa and learn about its historical significance.

2. Riva del Garda and Arco

- **Overview:** This tour combines two picturesque towns with a rich history.
- **Tour Highlights:**
  - **Riva del Garda:** Discover the historical center and visit the Apponale Tower.
  - **Arco:** Explore the ruins of Arco Castle and enjoy the beautiful gardens and architecture.

3. Brescia

- **Overview:** A short trip from Lake Garda, Brescia offers a wealth of historical sites.
- **Tour Highlights:**

- **Roman Forum:** Visit the remains of this ancient marketplace.
  - **Brescia Castle:** Tour the castle and enjoy panoramic views of the city.

Day Trips

1. Verona

- **Overview:** Known as the setting for Shakespeare's "Romeo and Juliet," Verona is just a short distance from Lake Garda.
- **Day Trip Highlights:**
  - **Juliet's House:** Visit the iconic balcony and explore the surrounding area.
  - **Arena di Verona:** Tour this ancient Roman amphitheater still used for concerts and operas.

2. Mantova (Mantua)
- **Overview:** A UNESCO World Heritage site, Mantova is rich in Renaissance art and architecture.

- Day Trip Highlights:
  - Palazzo Ducale: Explore the stunning rooms and art collection of the Ducal Palace.
  - Te Palace: Visit this beautiful villa designed by Giulio Romano.

3. Lake Iseo and Franciacorta
- Overview: This day trip combines the beauty of Lake Iseo with a visit to the famous Franciacorta wine region.

- Day Trip Highlights:
  - Boat Tour on Lake Iseo: Enjoy the scenic views and the charming island of Monte Isola.
  - Franciacorta Wine Tasting: Visit local wineries for tastings of renowned sparkling wines.

Tips for Historical Tours and Day Trips
- Plan Ahead: Check schedules and book tours in advance, especially during peak seasons.

- **Dress Comfortably:** Wear comfortable shoes, as many tours involve walking and exploring historic sites.
- **Stay Hydrated:** Bring water, especially for full-day trips, to stay refreshed.
- **Engage with Guides:** Don't hesitate to ask questions to gain deeper insights into the history and culture of the region.

Guided historical tours and day trips around Lake Garda offer a fascinating glimpse into the region's rich heritage. From ancient ruins to Renaissance art, these experiences provide a deeper understanding of the culture and history that define this beautiful area. Whether you're exploring quaint towns or majestic castles, Lake Garda's history awaits!

7.3 Boat and Ferry Tours

Exploring Lake Garda by boat is one of the best ways to appreciate its stunning landscapes, charming towns, and crystal-clear waters. Boat and ferry tours offer a unique perspective on the lake and allow visitors to access some of its most beautiful spots. Here's a guide to the various options available.

Types of Boat Tours
1. Ferry Services

- **Overview:** The lake is serviced by a reliable ferry system connecting major towns, making it easy to hop between destinations.
- **Key Routes:**
  - **Desenzano to Sirmione:** A short ferry ride to explore the historic sites of Sirmione.
  - **Riva del Garda to Limone:** Enjoy scenic views while traveling along the northern part of the lake.

2. Private Boat Rentals
- **Overview:** For a more personalized experience, consider renting a boat.
- **Options:**
  - **Motorboats:** Available for rent without a license (subject to size restrictions).
  - **Sailing Boats:** Perfect for those with sailing experience looking to explore at their own pace.

3. Guided Boat Tours
- **Overview:** These tours typically include a local guide who provides insights into the lake's history and attractions.
- **Highlights:**
  - **Sightseeing Tours:** Visit picturesque towns like Malcesine and Limone, often with stops for exploration.
  - **Sunset Cruises:** Enjoy a romantic evening on the water while watching the sunset over the mountains.

Popular Boat Tour Experiences

1. Garda Island (Isola del Garda)
- **Overview:** This private island is home to a stunning villa and beautiful gardens.
- **Tour Highlights:**
  - Guided tours of the villa and its historical gardens.
  - Scenic boat ride to and from the island.

2. The Olive Oil Route
- **Overview:** Some boat tours focus on the region's olive oil production.
- **Highlights:**
  - Visits to local olive oil mills.
  - Tastings paired with local wines.

3. Lake Garda Adventure Tours
- **Overview:** Combine boat tours with activities like swimming, snorkeling, or hiking.
- **Highlights:**
  - Explore secluded coves and beaches.

- Guided hiking tours on nearby trails accessible by boat.

Tips for Boat and Ferry Tours
- **Check Schedules:** Ferry and tour schedules can vary, especially in off-peak seasons. Always check in advance.
- **Book in Advance:** Popular tours, especially during peak season, may require advance booking to secure your spot.
- **Dress Appropriately:** Bring layers, as it can be cooler on the water, and don't forget sunscreen.
- **Bring Snacks and Drinks:** Pack refreshments for longer trips, especially on private rentals.

Boat and ferry tours on Lake Garda provide an unforgettable way to explore the region's natural beauty and cultural heritage. Whether you choose a leisurely ferry ride, a guided tour, or a private boat rental, the breathtaking views and charming towns along the lake are sure to create lasting memories. Embrace the adventure and discover the magic of Lake Garda from the water!

7.4 Cooking Classes and Culinary Experiences

Lake Garda is not only a feast for the eyes but also for the palate. The region is renowned for its rich culinary traditions, fresh ingredients, and local wines. Participating in cooking classes and culinary experiences allows visitors to immerse themselves in the local culture and learn how to create authentic Italian dishes. Here's a guide to the best culinary experiences around Lake Garda.

Cooking Classes

1. Traditional Italian Cooking
- **Overview:** Learn to prepare classic Italian dishes using fresh, local ingredients.

- **What to Expect:**
  - Hands-on experience making pasta, risotto, and sauces.
  - Emphasis on regional specialties, such as fish dishes and seasonal vegetables.

2. Cooking with Locals
- **Overview:** Enjoy a unique experience by cooking in a local's home.
- **Highlights:**
  - Personal interaction with local chefs who share family recipes and cooking secrets.
  - Often includes a meal shared with the host, enhancing the cultural experience.

3. Wine and Cooking Pairing Classes
- **Overview:** Combine the art of cooking with wine pairing.
- **What to Expect:**
  - Prepare dishes specifically designed to complement local wines.
  - Learn about wine selection and tasting techniques.

Culinary Experiences

1. Food Tours
- **Overview:** Explore the culinary landscape of Lake Garda through guided food tours.
- **Highlights:**
  - Sample local delicacies such as olive oil, cheese, and cured meats.
  - Visit markets, artisanal shops, and local producers.

2. Olive Oil Tasting
- **Overview:** Discover the famous olive oils of the region.
- **What to Expect:**
  - Tours of olive oil mills with tastings of various oils.
  - Learn about the production process and the importance of olive oil in Italian cuisine.

3. Market Visits and Cooking Classes

- **Overview:** Combine a market tour with a cooking class.
- **Highlights:**
   - Visit local markets to select fresh ingredients.
   - Prepare a meal using the ingredients sourced from the market.

Tips for Culinary Experiences

- **Book in Advance:** Popular classes and tours can fill up quickly, especially during peak seasons.
- **Dietary Preferences:** Inform instructors of any dietary restrictions or preferences beforehand.
- **Wear Comfortable Clothing:** Cooking can be messy, so dress appropriately and wear comfortable shoes.
- **Engage with Instructors:** Don't hesitate to ask questions and take notes to enhance your learning experience.

Cooking classes and culinary experiences around Lake Garda offer a delightful way to explore the region's rich food culture. From hands-on cooking lessons to wine and olive oil tastings, these experiences provide a deeper connection to the local traditions and flavors. Whether you're a seasoned cook or a curious beginner, you'll leave with new skills and unforgettable memories of Italian cuisine!

Chapter 8: Dining and Local Cuisine

8.1 Top Restaurants Around the Lake

Lake Garda is a culinary paradise, offering a diverse range of dining options that highlight the region's fresh ingredients and traditional recipes. Here's a guide to some of the top restaurants around the lake, each providing a unique dining experience.

1. Ristorante La Rucola (Sirmione)
- **Cuisine:** Italian, Mediterranean
- **Overview:** This restaurant is known for its elegant atmosphere and creative dishes made with local ingredients.
- **Highlights:**
  - Fresh seafood and homemade pasta.
  - Stunning views of Lake Garda from the terrace.

2. Trattoria Al Graspo (Bardolino)
- **Cuisine:** Traditional Italian
- **Overview:** A charming trattoria offering authentic regional dishes in a cozy setting.
- **Highlights:**
   - Specialties include risotto and local wines.
   - Friendly service and a welcoming vibe.

3. Osteria Da Bacco (Malcesine)
- **Cuisine:** Italian, Seafood
- **Overview:** Located in the historic center of Malcesine, this osteria is famous for its fresh seafood and rustic charm.
- **Highlights:**
  - Seasonal menu featuring local catch.
   - Outdoor seating with breathtaking lake views.

4. Ristorante Pizzeria Al Pescatore (Limone sul Garda)

- **Cuisine:** Italian, Pizzeria
- **Overview:** A family-run restaurant renowned for its delicious pizzas and traditional Italian dishes.
- **Highlights:**
    - Wood-fired pizzas and homemade desserts.
    - Beautiful terrace overlooking the lake.

5. Ristorante Il Fagiano (Riva del Garda)

- **Cuisine:** Italian, Gourmet
- **Overview:** A sophisticated restaurant focusing on gourmet Italian cuisine with a modern twist.
- **Highlights:**
    - Tasting menus featuring seasonal ingredients.
    - Extensive wine list with local selections.

6. Caffè Centrale (Desenzano del Garda)

- **Cuisine:** Café, Italian
- **Overview:** A popular spot for casual dining and people-watching in the heart of Desenzano.
- **Highlights:**
  - Delicious coffee, pastries, and light meals.
  - Perfect for a relaxed lunch or afternoon break.

7. Ristorante Villa Arcadio (Salò)

- **Cuisine:** Italian, Fine Dining
- **Overview:** Set in a historic villa, this restaurant offers an upscale dining experience with stunning lake views.
- **Highlights:**
  - Innovative dishes using fresh, local ingredients.
  - Romantic ambiance, ideal for special occasions.

Tips for Dining Around Lake Garda

- **Reservations:** Popular restaurants can get busy, especially in peak tourist season. Making reservations is recommended.
- **Local Specialties:** Don't miss trying local dishes such as tortellini di carne, risotto, and olive oil from the region.
- **Wine Pairings:** Ask for wine recommendations to complement your meal, as Lake Garda is home to excellent local wines.
- **Dining Hours:** Be aware that many restaurants have specific opening hours, with lunch typically served until 2:30 PM and dinner starting around 7 PM.

Dining around Lake Garda is a delightful experience, with a variety of restaurants offering something for every taste. From casual trattorias to elegant fine dining, the region's culinary scene reflects its rich traditions and local ingredients. Whether you're enjoying a leisurely meal by the lake or indulging in gourmet cuisine, Lake Garda promises to satisfy your culinary cravings!

8.2 Must-Try Dishes of the Garda Region

Lake Garda's culinary landscape is rich and diverse, reflecting its history and the abundance of local ingredients. Here's a guide to the must-try dishes that showcase the flavors of the Garda region.

1. Tortellini di Carne

- **Description:** These stuffed pasta parcels are filled with a mix of meats, typically including pork, beef, and spices.
- **Why Try It:** A delicious representation of local pasta-making traditions, often served in broth or with a rich sauce.

2. Risotto al Pesce

- **Description:** A creamy risotto made with fresh fish from the lake, such as perch or trout.

- **Why Try It:** This dish highlights the region's connection to the lake, offering a taste of fresh, local seafood.

3. Polenta

- **Description:** A traditional dish made from cornmeal, served creamy or sliced and grilled.
- **Why Try It:** Often paired with meats or stews, polenta is a staple in the region's cuisine, reflecting its rustic roots.

4. Caprese Salad

- **Description:** A simple yet flavorful salad made with fresh mozzarella, tomatoes, basil, and olive oil.
- **Why Try It:** This classic dish emphasizes the quality of local ingredients, particularly the region's renowned olive oil.

5. Sardine di Lago

- **Description:** Fresh sardines caught in Lake Garda, typically grilled or marinated.

- **Why Try It:** A local delicacy, these fish are often served as an appetizer, showcasing the lake's fresh produce.

6. Gnocchi di Patate
- **Description:** Soft potato dumplings, often served with a variety of sauces or in broth.
- **Why Try It:** These tender dumplings are a comforting dish, beloved for their versatility and rich flavor.

7. Baccalà Mantecato
- **Description:** A creamy spread made from salted cod, typically served on crostini or polenta.
- **Why Try It:** This dish reflects the influence of Venetian cuisine and is a popular appetizer in the region.

8. Local Wines
- **Description:** Lake Garda is home to several renowned wine varieties, including Bardolino and Lugana.
- **Why Try It:** Pairing local wines with your meal enhances the dining experience,

showcasing the region's agricultural richness.

Tips for Enjoying Local Cuisine

- **Ask for Recommendations:** Don't hesitate to ask locals or restaurant staff for their favorite dishes.
- **Try Seasonal Menus:** Many restaurants offer seasonal specials that highlight fresh, local ingredients.
- **Enjoy with Friends:** Many traditional meals are served family-style, encouraging sharing and conversation.

8.3 Olive Oil: The Culinary Staples

Lake Garda is celebrated not only for its stunning landscapes but also for its exceptional wine and olive oil production. These culinary staples play a vital role in the region's gastronomy, enhancing local dishes and enriching the dining experience.

Olive Oil of Lake Garda

1. Extra Virgin Olive Oil

- **Description:** Lake Garda produces high-quality extra virgin olive oil, renowned for its fruity flavor and low acidity.
- **Characteristics:**
  - **Varieties:** Primarily made from the Casaliva, Leccino, and Frantoio olives.
  - **Flavor Profile:** Fruity and slightly peppery, with a fresh aroma; ideal for drizzling, dipping, or cooking.

2. Olive Oil Tastings

- **Overview:** Many local producers offer tastings, allowing visitors to sample different oils and learn about the production process.
- **Experience:** Engage with local producers, explore the nuances of flavor,

and discover how to pair oils with various dishes.

Tips for Enjoying Wine and Olive Oil

- **Pairing:** Experiment with different wine and olive oil pairings to enhance your meals. For example, use a robust olive oil with grilled vegetables and a light white wine with fish.

- **Local Shops:** Visit local markets or shops to find artisanal wines and olive oils to bring home as souvenirs.

- **Attend Tastings:** Participate in guided wine and olive oil tastings to deepen your understanding of the region's offerings.

8.4 Best Gelato Spots

No visit to Lake Garda is complete without indulging in its renowned gelato. With its creamy texture and vibrant flavors, gelato is a beloved treat in the region. Here's a guide to some of the best gelato spots around Lake Garda.

1. Gelateria La Romana (Sirmione)

- **Overview:** Famous for its artisanal gelato made from high-quality ingredients.
- **Must-Try Flavors:** Stracciatella, pistachio, and seasonal fruit sorbets.
- **Ambiance:** Cozy and inviting, perfect for enjoying a scoop by the lakeside.

2. Gelateria Pasticceria Gigi (Bardolino)

- **Overview:** A local favorite known for its rich and creamy gelato.
- **Must-Try Flavors:** Chocolate fondente (dark chocolate) and nocciola (hazelnut).
- **Ambiance:** Friendly service and a charming outdoor seating area.

3. Gelateria Al Sole (Desenzano del Garda)

- **Overview:** Offers a wide range of traditional and innovative flavors.

- **Must-Try Flavors:** Mango, tiramisu, and their signature lemon basil.
- **Ambiance:** Bright and cheerful, with plenty of seating for enjoying your treat.

4. Gelateria La Dolce Vita (Malcesine)

- **Overview:** Known for its natural ingredients and authentic flavors.
- **Must-Try Flavors:** Fresh fruit sorbets and creamy gelato with local nuts.
- **Ambiance:** Picturesque views of the castle, ideal for a post-stroll treat.

5. Gelateria Arti e Mestieri (Riva del Garda)

- **Overview:** Combines traditional gelato-making techniques with modern flavors.
- **Must-Try Flavors:** Ricotta with figs and lavender honey.
- **Ambiance:** Artistic decor and a relaxed atmosphere, perfect for families.

6. Gelateria Nivola (Limone sul Garda)

- **Overview:** A charming gelateria known for its homemade gelato and sorbets.
- **Must-Try Flavors:** Lemon (made from local lemons) and dark chocolate.
- **Ambiance:** Quaint and welcoming, with lakeside seating options.

Tips for Enjoying Gelato

- **Sample Before You Order:** Don't hesitate to ask for samples to find your favorite flavor.
- **Try Seasonal Flavors:** Local gelaterias often offer flavors based on seasonal ingredients, so be sure to try them.
- **Pair with a Cono or Coppa:** Enjoy your gelato in a cone or cup for a classic experience.

Chapter 9: Shopping and Souvenirs

9.1 Local Markets and Artisan Shops

Lake Garda is not only a feast for the senses in terms of its natural beauty and cuisine but also a vibrant hub for shopping, especially when it comes to local markets and artisan shops. Here's a guide to some of the best spots to find unique souvenirs and local products.

Local Markets

1. Bardolino Market

- **When:** Every Wednesday morning
- **Overview:** This bustling market features a variety of stalls selling fresh produce, local cheeses, meats, and handmade crafts.

- **Highlights:** Look for local wines and olive oils to take home as souvenirs.

2. Sirmione Market

- **When:** Every Tuesday morning
- **Overview:** Located in the charming town of Sirmione, this market offers a mix of food, clothing, and artisanal products.
- **Highlights:** Don't miss the handmade ceramics and traditional Italian textiles.

3. Desenzano del Garda Market

- **When:** Every Sunday morning
- **Overview:** A large market with a wide range of goods, from fresh fruits and vegetables to clothing and accessories.
- **Highlights:** Great place to find local handicrafts and souvenirs.

Artisan Shops

1. Bottega del Vino (Bardolino)

- **Overview:** A specialty shop dedicated to local wines and spirits.
- **What to Buy:** Bottles of Bardolino wine and unique wine-related gifts.
- **Tip:** Ask for recommendations to find the perfect local vintage.

2. Laboratorio Artigiano (Malcesine)

- **Overview:** This artisan workshop specializes in handmade pottery and ceramics.
- **What to Buy:** Beautifully crafted dishes, bowls, and decorative items.
- **Tip:** Each piece is unique, making it a perfect souvenir.

3. Olive Oil Shop (Limone sul Garda)

- **Overview:** A local shop focused on high-quality olive oils produced in the region.
- **What to Buy:** Extra virgin olive oil, flavored oils, and olive oil-based cosmetics.
- **Tip:** Consider a tasting to find your favorite oil.

4. La Bottega del Gusto (Riva del Garda)

- **Overview:** A gourmet shop offering a variety of local delicacies.
- **What to Buy:** Local cheeses, cured meats, and artisanal pasta.
- **Tip:** Perfect for creating a picnic basket or gifts for food lovers.

Tips for Shopping

- **Bargaining:** While not common in artisan shops, some markets may allow for negotiation, especially for larger purchases.

- **Local Products:** Focus on buying items that are unique to the region, such as wines, olive oils, and handmade crafts.
- **Support Local Artisans:** Purchasing directly from artisans helps support the local economy and often ensures you receive a high-quality product.

Shopping around Lake Garda offers a delightful experience, from vibrant local markets to charming artisan shops. Whether you're looking for delicious local products or unique handcrafted souvenirs, the region provides plenty of options to take a piece of its charm home with you. Enjoy exploring the shops and markets!

9.2 Best Places for Wine and Olive Oil Shopping

Lake Garda is renowned for its exquisite wines and high-quality olive oils, making it a fantastic destination for enthusiasts looking to bring home a taste of the region. Here's a guide to some of the best places to shop for these culinary treasures.

Wine Shops

1. Enoteca Regionale del Bardolino (Bardolino)

- **Overview:** A dedicated wine shop showcasing the best of Bardolino wines.
- **What to Buy:** A wide selection of Bardolino DOC wines, including both red and rosé varieties.
- **Tip:** Ask for tasting options to discover your favorite wine before purchasing.

2. Cantina del Garda (Desenzano del Garda)

- **Overview:** A cooperative that offers a variety of wines from local vineyards.
- **What to Buy:** Lugana white wines and Chiaretto rosés.

- **Tip:** Look for special offers on mixed cases for a great value.

3. Vigna del Sole (Riva del Garda)

- **Overview:** A charming wine shop featuring local wines and gourmet products.
- **What to Buy:** Unique local blends and organic wines.
- **Tip:** Inquire about wine tours for a deeper understanding of the region's winemaking.

Olive Oil Shops

1. Frantoio di Riva del Garda (Riva del Garda)

- **Overview:** An olive oil mill that produces high-quality extra virgin olive oil.
- **What to Buy:** Freshly pressed olive oil and flavored oils.
- **Tip:** Participate in an olive oil tasting to explore different varieties.

2. Oleificio (Limone sul Garda)

- **Overview:** A local oil mill known for its premium olive oils.
- **What to Buy:** Bottles of traditional olive oil and artisanal products like tapenade.
- **Tip:** Look for gift sets that combine olive oil with local spices.

3. La Bottega dell'Olio (Sirmione)

- **Overview:** A boutique olive oil shop specializing in local products.
- **What to Buy:** Extra virgin olive oil and gourmet food items.
- **Tip:** Check for cooking classes that focus on using olive oil in various dishes.

Tips for Wine and Olive Oil Shopping

- **Ask for Pairing Suggestions:** Store staff can provide valuable advice on pairing wines and oils with food.

- **Consider Gift Sets:** Many shops offer curated gift sets that make great souvenirs for friends and family.
- **Check for Local Tastings:** Some places host tastings, allowing you to sample before buying.

Shopping for wine and olive oil in Lake Garda is a delightful experience, with numerous shops offering quality products that capture the region's essence. Whether you're a connoisseur or a casual enthusiast, you'll find plenty of options to satisfy your cravings and bring home a piece of Lake Garda's culinary heritage. Enjoy your shopping adventure!

9.3 Fashion Boutiques and Shopping Districts

Lake Garda is not only a destination for natural beauty and culinary delights but also a vibrant shopping scene with a mix of local boutiques and stylish shopping districts.

Here's a guide to the best places to indulge in some retail therapy.

Fashion Boutiques

1. Boutique Azzurra (Sirmione)

- **Overview:** A chic boutique featuring a curated selection of Italian and international fashion brands.
- **What to Find:** Elegant clothing, accessories, and unique jewelry pieces.
- **Tip:** Look for seasonal sales to snag stylish items at a discount.

2. La Maison (Bardolino)

- **Overview:** A local boutique known for its trendy and contemporary fashion.
- **What to Find:** Stylish outfits for both men and women, along with accessories.
- **Tip:** Ask the staff for styling advice to create the perfect look.

3. Cappuccino (Desenzano del Garda)

- **Overview:** A fashionable boutique offering a wide range of casual and formal wear.
- **What to Find:** Italian brands, shoes, and handbags.
- **Tip:** Check out their collection of local designer pieces that you won't find elsewhere.

Shopping Districts

1. Via Giuseppe Mazzini (Bardolino)

- **Overview:** The main shopping street in Bardolino, lined with boutiques, cafes, and artisan shops.
- **What to Expect:** A variety of fashion, home goods, and souvenirs.
- **Tip:** Explore side streets for hidden gems and unique finds.

2. Piazza Malvezzi (Desenzano del Garda)

- **Overview:** A bustling square surrounded by shops and cafes, perfect for a leisurely shopping experience.
- **What to Expect:** A mix of high-street brands and local boutiques.
- **Tip:** Enjoy a coffee at a nearby cafe after shopping to soak up the atmosphere.

3. Corso Italia (Riva del Garda)

- **Overview:** The main thoroughfare in Riva del Garda, featuring a mix of fashion boutiques and lifestyle stores.
- **What to Expect:** Trendy apparel, local crafts, and artisanal products.
- **Tip:** Look for seasonal markets and pop-up shops that often take place here.

Tips for Fashion Shopping

- **Try Before You Buy:** Many boutiques will allow you to try on clothes, so take advantage of fitting rooms.

- **Shop Local:** Support local designers and artisans by choosing unique, handcrafted items.
- **Keep an Eye Out for Sales:** Look for end-of-season sales or holiday discounts for great deals.

Lake Garda offers a delightful shopping experience, from fashionable boutiques to charming shopping districts. Whether you're searching for the latest trends or unique local finds, the region provides ample opportunities to refresh your wardrobe and take home a slice of Italian style. Enjoy exploring the fashion scene!

Chapter 10: Day Trips and Excursions

10.1 Verona: The City of Romeo and Juliet

Verona, famous as the setting for Shakespeare's "Romeo and Juliet," is a charming city steeped in history, culture, and romance. Just a short trip from Lake Garda, it makes for an ideal day trip. Here's what to see and do while exploring this enchanting city.

Highlights of Verona

1. Juliet's House (Casa di Giulietta)
- **Overview:** A must-visit for fans of the tragic love story, this 14th-century house features a famous balcony.
- **What to Do:** Take a photo on the balcony and explore the museum inside. Don't forget to leave a love note on the walls.

2. Verona Arena
- **Overview:** This well-preserved Roman amphitheater dates back to AD 30 and is still used for concerts and operas today.
- **What to Do:** Take a guided tour to learn about its history and architecture. If possible, catch a performance for a memorable experience.

3. Piazza delle Erbe
- **Overview:** The vibrant heart of Verona, this lively square is surrounded by picturesque buildings and bustling markets.
- **What to Do:** Enjoy a coffee at one of the outdoor cafes, browse the market stalls, and admire the historic architecture.

4. Castelvecchio and Ponte Scaligero
- **Overview:** A medieval fortress and bridge offering stunning views of the city.
- **What to Do:** Visit the museum inside the castle, then stroll across the bridge for picturesque views of the Adige River.

5. Basilica di San Zeno
- **Overview:** A beautiful Romanesque church known for its impressive architecture and artwork.
- **What to Do:** Explore the stunning interiors and the famous triptych by Andrea Mantegna.

Tips for Visiting Verona
- **Transportation:** The city is easily accessible by train from Lake Garda, with regular services to Verona Porta Nuova station.
- **Walking:** Verona is a pedestrian-friendly city, so wear comfortable shoes for exploring its charming streets.
- **Timing:** Start your day early to make the most of your visit and avoid crowds at popular attractions.

A day trip to Verona offers a perfect blend of romance, history, and culture. From the iconic Juliet's House to the impressive Verona Arena, there's something for everyone to enjoy. Make sure to soak in the vibrant atmosphere and create unforgettable memories in this captivating city.

10.2 Venice: A Magical Day by the Canals

Venice, with its stunning canals, historic architecture, and vibrant culture, is a must-visit destination just a few hours from Lake Garda. A day trip to this enchanting city promises a unique experience filled with beauty and charm. Here's how to make the most of your visit to Venice.

Highlights of Venice

1. St. Mark's Basilica (Basilica di San Marco)
- **Overview:** This iconic cathedral is known for its stunning mosaics and impressive architecture.

- **What to Do:** Explore the ornate interiors and climb to the balcony for a breathtaking view of St. Mark's Square.

2. Piazza San Marco
- **Overview:** The main square of Venice, surrounded by historic buildings and bustling cafes.
- **What to Do:** Enjoy a coffee at one of the outdoor cafes while listening to live music. Don't miss the Campanile (bell tower) for panoramic views.

3. Grand Canal
- **Overview:** The main waterway of Venice, lined with magnificent palaces and historic buildings.
- **What to Do:** Take a Vaporetto (water bus) ride along the Grand Canal to see the city from the water. Consider a gondola ride for a classic Venetian experience.

4. Rialto Bridge (Ponte di Rialto)

- **Overview:** One of the most famous bridges in Venice, known for its stunning views and vibrant market.
- **What to Do:** Walk across the bridge for picturesque views of the Grand Canal and visit the nearby Rialto Market for fresh produce and local delicacies.

5. Murano and Burano Islands

- **Overview:** These nearby islands are famous for glassmaking (Murano) and colorful houses (Burano).
- **What to Do:** Take a short boat trip to explore the islands, watch glassblowing demonstrations in Murano, and stroll through Burano's charming streets.

Tips for Visiting Venice

- **Transportation:** Trains from Lake Garda to Venice are frequent, with the journey taking about 2 to 2.5 hours. Arrive early to maximize your day.

- **Walking:** Venice is best explored on foot, so wear comfortable shoes and be prepared for some walking on cobblestone streets.
- **Best Time to Visit:** Early mornings or late afternoons are ideal to avoid crowds and capture stunning photos.

A day in Venice is like stepping into a dream, filled with breathtaking sights and unforgettable experiences. From the majestic St. Mark's Basilica to the serene canals, Venice offers a magical atmosphere that captivates every visitor. Embrace the charm of this unique city and create lasting memories on your journey.

10.3 Dolomites: Exploring the Mountain Range

The Dolomites, a UNESCO World Heritage site, are known for their breathtaking landscapes, dramatic peaks, and outdoor activities. Just a short drive from Lake Garda, this stunning mountain range offers a perfect day trip for nature lovers and adventure seekers. Here's how to make the most of your visit to the Dolomites.

Highlights of the Dolomites

1. Cortina d'Ampezzo
- **Overview:** Known as the "Queen of the Dolomites," this charming town is a hub for skiing and outdoor activities.
- **What to Do:** Stroll through the picturesque streets, enjoy shopping, and savor local cuisine at one of the many restaurants.

2. Lago di Braies (Pragser Wildsee)
- **Overview:** A stunning alpine lake famous for its turquoise waters and surrounding mountains.
- **What to Do:** Take a leisurely walk around the lake, rent a rowboat, or simply relax and enjoy the breathtaking scenery.

3. Seceda
- **Overview:** A stunning plateau offering panoramic views of the Dolomites.
- **What to Do:** Take the cable car up for hiking trails that cater to all levels, with options ranging from easy walks to challenging hikes.

4. Val Gardena
- **Overview:** A picturesque valley known for its beautiful landscapes and outdoor activities.
- **What to Do:** Explore charming villages like Ortisei and Selva, and enjoy hiking, mountain biking, or simply taking in the stunning views.

5. Tre Cime di Lavaredo
- **Overview:** One of the most iconic mountain formations in the Dolomites.
- **What to Do:** Hike around the three peaks for incredible views and photo opportunities. The loop trail offers various vantage points for stunning panoramas.

Tips for Visiting the Dolomites

- **Transportation:** It's best to have a car for flexibility in exploring the region. Many scenic drives are available, showcasing the stunning landscapes.

- **Timing:** Start your day early to make the most of your time in the mountains and to enjoy popular spots before they get crowded.

- **Weather:** The weather can change rapidly in the mountains, so dress in layers and be prepared for varying conditions.

A trip to the Dolomites offers an unforgettable experience, with stunning scenery and a wealth of outdoor activities. Whether you're hiking, relaxing by a lake, or enjoying the charm of mountain towns, the Dolomites provide a perfect escape into nature. Embrace the beauty of this magnificent mountain range and create lasting memories in the heart of the Alps.

10.4 Milan: Fashion and Culture

Milan, Italy's fashion capital, is a vibrant city that seamlessly blends style, art, and history. Just a short journey from Lake Garda, it makes for an exciting day trip filled with cultural experiences and shopping opportunities. Here's how to explore the best of Milan.

Highlights of Milan

1. Duomo di Milano
- **Overview:** The magnificent cathedral is one of the largest Gothic churches in the world.
- **What to Do:** Climb to the rooftop for stunning views of the city and admire the intricate architecture. Don't forget to explore the interiors and the beautiful stained glass windows.

2. Galleria Vittorio Emanuele II

- **Overview:** A stunning shopping arcade that showcases luxury brands and elegant cafes.
- **What to Do:** Stroll through the gallery, enjoy some gelato, and take a photo with the iconic bull mosaic for good luck.

3. Castello Sforzesco

- **Overview:** A historic castle that houses several museums and art collections.
- **What to Do:** Explore the castle grounds and visit the museums, including the Museum of Ancient Art and the Pinacoteca. The surrounding Sempione Park is perfect for a relaxing stroll.

4. Santa Maria delle Grazie

- **Overview:** Home to Leonardo da Vinci's masterpiece, "The Last Supper."
- **What to Do:** Book tickets in advance to view this iconic mural. The church itself is a beautiful example of Renaissance architecture.

5. Navigli District

- **Overview:** A picturesque area known for its canals, trendy boutiques, and vibrant nightlife.
- **What to Do:** Explore the charming streets, visit the local shops, and enjoy aperitivo at one of the many waterfront bars.

Tips for Visiting Milan

- **Transportation:** Milan has an efficient public transport system, including trams and metro. Consider a day pass for convenient travel.
- **Timing:** Start your day early to avoid crowds at major attractions and allow time for leisurely exploration.
- **Shopping:** If you're interested in fashion, explore the Quadrilatero della Moda, Milan's high-end shopping district.

Chapter 11: Practical Information and Tips

11.1 Budgeting for Your Trip

When planning your journey to Lake Garda and its surrounding attractions, budgeting is essential for a smooth and enjoyable experience. Here are key considerations to help you manage your finances effectively.

Estimated Daily Expenses

1. Accommodation
- **Budget Hotels/Hostels:** €50 - €100 per night
- **Mid-range Hotels:** €100 - €200 per night
- **Luxury Hotels:** €200+ per night

2. Food and Dining
- **Budget Meals:** €10 - €20 (pizza, sandwiches)
- **Mid-range Restaurants:** €20 - €50 (local cuisine, multi-course meals)

- **Fine Dining:** €50+ (gourmet experiences)

3. Transportation
- **Local Transport:**
  - **Buses/Trains:** €2 - €10 per ride
  - **Day passes:** €5 - €15
- **Rental Cars:** €30 - €70 per day (plus fuel and insurance)

4. Attractions and Activities
- **Museums and Sites:** €5 - €15 (entry fees)
- **Guided Tours:** €30 - €100 (depending on the tour length and inclusions)
- **Outdoor Activities:** Prices vary (e.g., ski passes, boat rentals)

Budgeting Tips
- **Plan Ahead:** Research and book accommodations and activities in advance to secure better rates.
- **Travel Off-Peak:** Consider visiting in the shoulder seasons (spring or fall) for lower prices and fewer crowds.

- **Eat Like a Local:** Try trattorias or street food for authentic and affordable meals.
- **Use Public Transport:** Save on transportation costs by utilizing local buses and trains instead of taxis.

Currency and Payment

- **Currency:** Euro (€)
- **Credit Cards:** Widely accepted, but carry some cash for small purchases and in rural areas.
- **ATMs:** Available in cities and towns; check for foreign transaction fees from your bank.

Budgeting for your trip to Lake Garda and nearby destinations doesn't have to be daunting. By planning your expenses and making informed choices, you can enjoy a memorable experience without breaking the bank. Remember to keep some flexibility in your budget for spontaneous adventures!

11.2 Safety and Emergency Contacts

When traveling, it's important to prioritize safety and be prepared for any situation. Here's a detailed guide on how to stay safe while visiting Lake Garda and the surrounding areas, along with essential emergency contacts.

General Safety Tips

1. Stay Aware of Your Surroundings

- Be vigilant in crowded places, especially in tourist hotspots where pickpockets might operate.

- Keep your belongings close and secure.

2. Use Reliable Transportation

- Opt for licensed taxis or reputable ride-sharing services.

- If using public transport, keep an eye on your bags and personal items.

3. Emergency Services

- Dial 112 for general emergencies (medical, fire, police).

- This number is valid across the EU.

4. Travel Insurance
- Consider purchasing travel insurance that covers medical emergencies, trip cancellations, and lost belongings.

Health and Medical Information
1. Local Healthcare Facilities
- **Hospitals:** Major cities like Brescia and Verona have well-equipped hospitals.
- **Pharmacies:** Available in towns and cities; look for a green cross sign. Many pharmacists speak English.

2. Emergency Medical Assistance
- In case of a medical emergency, call 112 or go directly to the nearest hospital or clinic.

3. Vaccinations and Health Precautions
- Make sure routine vaccinations are up to date. Check if any additional vaccinations are recommended before your trip.

Emergency Contacts

1. Local Emergency Services
  - **Police:** 112
  - **Ambulance:** 118
  - **Fire Department:** 115

2. Embassies and Consulates
  - **United States:**
    - **Embassy in Rome:** +39 06 46741
    - **Consulate in Milan:** +39 02 631681
  - **United Kingdom:**
    - **Embassy in Rome:** +39 06 4220 0001
    - **Consulate in Milan:** +39 02 7234 3000
  - **Canada:**
    - **Embassy in Rome:** +39 06 8519 2000
  - **Australia:**
    - **Embassy in Rome:** +39 06 8527 0001

3. Local Contacts
  - **Tourist Information Centers:** Available in major towns around Lake

Garda; they can provide assistance and resources.

   - **Accommodations:** Your hotel or hostel can help in emergencies and provide local advice.

Additional Safety Precautions
1. Natural Hazards
   - Be aware of weather conditions, especially if engaging in outdoor activities like hiking or skiing.
   - Always follow local advice regarding safety during extreme weather events.

2. Road Safety
   - If driving, familiarize yourself with local traffic laws. Always wear a seatbelt and avoid using a mobile phone while driving.

3. Wildlife and Nature
   - If hiking or exploring nature, stay on marked trails, and be cautious of local wildlife.

 Staying safe while traveling to Lake Garda and surrounding areas requires awareness and preparation. Keep these safety tips and emergency contact numbers handy to ensure a worry-free trip. By being informed and cautious, you can fully enjoy the beauty and culture of this stunning region.

11.3 Traveling with Kids and Family

Traveling with kids and family can be a rewarding experience, especially in a family-friendly destination like Lake Garda. Here's a comprehensive guide to make your trip enjoyable and stress-free.

Family-Friendly Activities
1. Theme Parks
   - **Gardaland:** One of Italy's largest amusement parks, featuring rides and attractions for all ages.
   - **Movieland Park:** A fun film-themed park with live shows, rides, and interactive experiences.

2. Water Activities

- **Beach Days:** Enjoy family-friendly beaches like Spiaggia di Peschiera, which have shallow waters perfect for young children.

- **Boat Trips:** Take a scenic boat ride on the lake, which can be exciting for kids and offers beautiful views.

3. Nature Exploration

- **Hiking Trails:** Choose easy trails suitable for families, such as those around Limone sul Garda or the paths near Malcesine.

- **Gardens and Parks:** Visit parks like the Giardino Botanico Fondazione André Heller for a leisurely stroll among beautiful plants.

Tips for Traveling with Kids

1. Pack Smart

- Bring essential items like snacks, water, sunscreen, hats, and any necessary medications.

- Consider a lightweight stroller for younger children, as some areas may have cobblestone streets.

2. Plan Your Itinerary Wisely

- Balance sightseeing with downtime to avoid overwhelming your kids.
- Include activities that cater to various age groups and interests.

3. Dining with Kids

- Look for family-friendly restaurants that offer kids' menus and high chairs.
- Try local gelato shops for a sweet treat that kids will love.

Accommodation

1. Family-Friendly Hotels

- Choose accommodations that offer family rooms or suites. Many hotels provide amenities like cribs, play areas, and pools.
- Consider vacation rentals for more space and a kitchen to prepare meals.

2. Location Matters

- Stay in areas that are convenient to attractions and amenities, reducing travel time and making it easier to return to your accommodation for breaks.

Safety Considerations

1. Child Safety

- Keep a close eye on children, especially near water and busy areas.
- Teach kids about road safety and crossing streets.

2. Emergency Preparedness

- Familiarize yourself with local emergency contacts and nearby medical facilities.
- Carry a first-aid kit for minor injuries.

Traveling with kids and family can be a delightful adventure at Lake Garda. By planning ahead and choosing activities that suit all ages, you can create lasting memories together. Embrace the beauty of the region and enjoy quality time with your loved ones!

11.4 Accessibility and Travel Tips for Seniors

Traveling to Lake Garda can be a wonderful experience for seniors, offering stunning scenery, rich culture, and a variety of activities. Here's a comprehensive guide to ensure a comfortable and enjoyable trip.

Accessibility Considerations

1. Transportation

   - **Public Transport:** Many buses and trains are accessible, but check schedules in advance. Some routes may have limited accessibility.

   - **Taxis:** Look for taxi companies that offer vehicles equipped for wheelchair access.

   - **Rental Cars:** Consider renting a car with hand controls if needed; some companies provide adapted vehicles.

2. Accommodations

   - **Choose Accessible Hotels:** Look for hotels that offer wheelchair-accessible rooms, elevators, and facilities.

- **Location:** Stay in central areas to minimize travel distance to attractions and amenities.

3. Attraction Accessibility
- **Research Attractions:** Many popular sites, such as the Duomo in Milan and the gardens at Gardaland, are equipped with ramps and accessible paths. Verify accessibility options prior to visiting.

Travel Tips for Seniors
1. Plan Your Itinerary
- **Pace Yourself:** Avoid cramming too many activities into one day. Allow time for relaxation and breaks.
- **Prioritize Activities:** Focus on attractions that interest you most and that are also accessible.

2. Pack Wisely
- **Essentials:** Bring necessary medications, comfortable shoes, and lightweight clothing suitable for the weather.

- **Mobility Aids:** If needed, bring a walking cane, walker, or wheelchair. Check with airlines about policies for traveling with mobility aids.

3. Health and Safety
   - **Stay Hydrated:** Drink plenty of water, especially during outdoor activities.
   - **Emergency Contacts:** Keep a list of emergency contacts, including local medical facilities. Familiarize yourself with local healthcare options.

4. Dining Options
   - **Choose Comfortable Restaurants:** Look for places with accessible seating and a relaxed atmosphere. Many restaurants in tourist areas are equipped to accommodate seniors.

5. Communication
   - **Language:** While many Italians speak English, learning a few basic Italian phrases

can enhance your experience and make communication easier.

- **Travel Insurance:** Consider getting travel insurance that covers health emergencies and trip cancellations.

With thoughtful planning and consideration, seniors can enjoy a rewarding trip to Lake Garda. By focusing on accessibility and comfort, you can explore this beautiful region at your own pace, creating memorable experiences along the way. Enjoy your travels!

11.5 Local Contacts

Having a list of local contacts can enhance your travel experience in Lake Garda and provide essential support during your visit. Here's a comprehensive guide to important local contacts you may need.

Emergency Services

- **General Emergency Number:** 112 (for police, fire, and medical emergencies)
- **Ambulance:** 118

- **Fire Department:** 115
- **Local Police:** Contact the nearest police station for assistance.

Medical Services
- **Hospitals:**
  - **Ospedale di Desenzano del Garda:** +39 030 999 6111
  - **Ospedale Civile di Brescia:** +39 030 399 1111
- **Pharmacies (Farmacia):**
  - **Farmacia Comunale (Desenzano):** +39 030 914 4736
  - **Farmacia del Lago (Sirmione):** +39 030 990 1986

Tourist Information Centers
- **Desenzano del Garda:**
  - **Address:** Via Roma, 54, 25015 Desenzano del Garda
  - **Phone:** +39 030 999 1950
- **Sirmione:**
  - **Address:** Piazza Carducci, 1, 25019 Sirmione

- **Phone:** +39 030 916 188

- **Riva del Garda:**
  - **Address:** Via Giuseppe Mazzini, 1, 38066 Riva del Garda
  - **Phone:** +39 0464 554 999

Transportation Contacts
- **Local Bus Services:**
  - **Navigazione Lago di Garda (Ferry Services):** +39 0365 500 203
  - **Buses:** Consult the Trasporti Pubblici Provincia di Brescia website for schedules.
- **Taxi Services:**
  - **Taxi Desenzano:** +39 030 919 000
  - **Taxi Sirmione:** +39 348 460 8888

Embassy and Consulate Contacts
- **United States Embassy (Rome):** +39 06 46741
- **British Embassy (Rome):** +39 06 4220 0001
- **Canadian Embassy (Rome):** +39 06 8519 2000

- **Australian Embassy (Rome):** +39 06 8527 0001

Local Tour Operators
- **Lake Garda Tours:** +39 045 620 3040
- **Garda Outdoors (Outdoor Activities):** +39 347 422 3212

Keeping these local contacts handy will help ensure a smooth and enjoyable trip to Lake Garda. Whether you need assistance, information, or support, knowing who to reach out to can enhance your travel experience and provide peace of mind. Enjoy your time in this beautiful region!